simply japanese

simply japanese

modern cooking for the healthy home

yoko arimoto

photographs by fumihiko watanabe

KODANSHA INTERNATIONAL
Tokyo • New York • London

Distributed in the United States by Kodansha America LLC, and in the United Kingdom and continental Europe by Kodansha Europe Ltd.

Published by Kodansha International Ltd., 17-14 Otowa 1-chome, Bunkyo-ku, Tokyo 112-8652.

ISBN 978-4-7700-3102-0

First edition, 2010
18 17 16 15 14 13 12 11 10 10 9 8 7 6 5 4 3 2 1

Library of Congress Cataloging-in-Publication Data

Arimoto, Yoko.
Simply Japanese : modern cooking for the healthy home / Yoko Arimoto ; photography, Fumihiko Watanabe.
p. cm.
Includes bibliographical references and index.
ISBN 978-4-7700-3102-0
1. Cookery, Japanese--Recipes. I. Title.
TX724.5.J3A785 2010
641.5952--dc22

2009046007

www.kodansha-intl.com

contents

introduction

Even as a child I was aware of my parents' concern for what we ate, especially at home. My father was born to a traditional soy sauce and sake brewer from Fukushima in the north of Japan, where the remnants of the old feudalistic family system still existed. My mother was the daughter of a doctor from Nagasaki in the south of Japan, where the culture, influenced by the West through trade with Europe, was more open. Despite coming from such different backgrounds, my parents had the same ideas about what we ate at home. They would pay special attention to the quality and healthiness of the ingredients they used, buying vegetables that were crisp and wholesome from neighbors, so I grew up loving vegetables as a child.

We lived in a suburb of Tokyo, so it was my father's job to buy good bread and cheese in the city, and freshly caught fish at Tsukiji, the famous Tokyo fish market. In those days, a trip to Tokyo was still a big event! We would also dine out once in a while in the city. My father sometimes took us to famous tempura restaurants, and my mother always wanted to sit at the counter and look at what the cooks were doing. She brought the tips and techniques she learned back to her home kitchen. My childhood is full of happy memories of food, and I am deeply thankful for the way my parents raised me.

When I started my own family and spent a great deal of time cooking, I couldn't help thinking how creative and fun cooking at home can be, just like my mother must have done. Along with my three daughters, I took care of nieces and nephews, and I enjoyed the liveliness of cooking: making *bento* lunch boxes, baking bread, preparing preserved foods, and so on. My family also had a lot of guests over for dinner, and it is during those years that I learned how to make meals in a systematic, effective way. I wanted to cook the best meals that I could, but with great care, and without spending a lot of money. At the same time, the meals needed to have a good balance of nutrition to maintain my family's and guest's health. To achieve all of this I had to be creative. As I gained knowledge and experience of food and cooking, I found new ideas coming out of me easily. I enjoyed every minute of being a housewife.

One day, our house was chosen by an interior decorating magazine to feature in an article. After the article was published, I was surprised to receive continuous requests for interviews on the interior, décor, and dishes I had collected. I also made some simple meals to serve with my tableware, and was fortunate enough to have a number of interviews on my food also. I decided to publish a cookbook, and clearly developed a taste for it, as I ended up publishing about 100 books in twenty years! The cookbooks range from quick meals for working singles, to elaborate Japanese cuisine for entertaining family and friends, to more specific books about cooking tools, sun-dried vegetables, and olive oil (since I eventually found a house in Italy and spent part of my time there). But I never felt I was working too hard; I simply let every book grow naturally out of my real life.

My ideas are still pouring out like a fountain, because, I think, I have always had a message for people: I deeply feel that cooking at home is the healthiest way to live, and I believe that wholesome, nutritious food can only be achieved by choosing the finest, natural ingredients. I would love to see more people cook at home for their friends and family, and for themselves. I have followed in my mother's footsteps and devoted a considerable amount of time to cooking at home, and have come to understand that taking a sincere approach to one's cooking leads to a naturally healthy life in both body and mind. It's also fun to get to know the ingredients you are going to eat, by searching them out, getting a feel for them, and preparing them. Choosing local fresh ingredients and seasonings prepared with great care and no artificial additives is a thoughtful, healthy approach to what you eat. And believe me, good-quality ingredients simply taste best and surprisingly improve your cooking.

Although Japan's diet has changed, home cooking in Japan—the country with the longest average life expectancy in the world—is still based on plenty of brightly colored vegetables, seaweed, fish, grains, miso and other fermented foods, plus a little meat. Eating healthily is not the same as eating low-calorie food. A good balance in calories and nutrition creates a slim and healthy body without harsh dieting.

Outside Japan, I have witnessed the worldwide explosion in the popularity of sushi develop into a more general interest in Japanese cuisine, and I have learned about many wonderful foods around the world that I would not have encountered in Japan. I have also gained opportunities to entertain friends with Japanese cooking—all of which brought me to the question of how to cook Japanese food outside Japan.

After experimenting a little, I found that I didn't need to go out of my way to find much the same ingredients abroad as in Japan. Basic Japanese seasonings such as soy sauce and rice vinegar are now available in supermarkets, as well as through the Internet. Besides, each country has its own fine foods that reach their peak at the right season, and I was able to turn those foods into Japanese cooking in my own way. Once I thought about it, the fundamentals were exactly the same as when I was in Japan—to cook as simply as possible, using available seasonings and fresh local ingredients. With a few well-kept basic utensils, some knowledge, and the desire to eat healthily, anyone can cook the Japanese way.

This book is full of modern Japanese food, the kind we Japanese eat every day. It's the food I've made for my family and friends, including Westerners, who all appreciate natural, good taste. If this book helps bring healthy, delicious Japanese home cooking to your daily table and adds even just a little to your life, then I couldn't be happier.

Yoko Arimoto, 2010, Tokyo

有元葉子

at the table

The Japanese formula for an ideal, well-balanced meal is expressed by the phrase, "*ichiju sansai,*" which means soup and three dishes (and rice; there's always rice). Soup supplies fluids and salt, the three other dishes provide protein, fiber, and vitamins, and rice provides energy-giving carbohydrates. Everything is usually served at the same time—the soup is not a prelude, but an accompaniment, and the three dishes are small portions, enough to finish in three or four mouthfuls. The idea is not to fill up on one kind of food, but to eat smaller amounts of a variety of foods.

One of the three dishes is the main dish, typically fish, meat, or tofu. The other two are side dishes: vegetables, seaweed, beans, or other ingredients rich in fiber, minerals, and vitamins. Many believe the secret to Japanese longevity is the tradition of making meals with the right nutritional balance. This sense of nutrition, developed by close daily attention to the healthiness of what we eat, has been naturally passed down from generation to generation in kitchens all over the country.

Japanese nutrition is not anything complicated or challenging. If you tend to have a lot of meat in your diet, then slightly reduce the amount of meat that you eat at one meal, and replace it with a few different vegetables. Do not fill up only on fried chicken, for example, but add a few side dishes from this book, like Crunchy Vegetable Batons with Roasted Sesame Oil Dressing, or Grand Vegetable Platter with Onion Vinegar Dressing. Even some corn-on-the-cob or roast squash will do. It is also important to cook vegetables along with meat. Recipes in this book, like Pan-roasted Duck Breast with *Mizuna* Greens, or Simmered Pork Shoulder and Cabbage with Dijon Mustard, make satisfying main dishes.

Tableware

I'm very fond of round, white plates, both for their versatility and for the clean, formal look they bring to a table. But there are only so

many ways to arrange food on them, and very often the foods you worked so hard to prepare end up looking much the same. In Japanese cuisine, appearance is as important as taste, so we exercise our utmost ingenuity to match food with dishes of just the right shape and color. Bowls are important, too, since many foods are served in a broth. Japanese dishes come in a wide range of materials, from porcelain and earthenware to lacquered wood, and we take full advantage of this variety to dress our tables according to the season.

While it may be difficult to obtain authentic lacquerware outside of Japan, you should at least find a miso soup bowl made with genuine lacquer. Miso soup is not eaten with a spoon, but drunk directly from the bowl. The warm, slightly yielding feel of lacquered wood on your lips is essential to the experience of drinking miso soup. A standard bowl measures about 4½ in. (11 cm) in diameter and will hold a modest cup (about 200 ml); a standard rice bowl has about the same diameter. Both bowls are intended to be held in the hand while eating with chopsticks, so when looking for the right one, experiment by picking them up and holding them in your hand. This will help you select the size and material that feel most comfortable.

Most of the recipes in this book have been photographed on serving platters. At my home, where I receive many guests, I serve rice and miso soup individually, but usually set other foods on the table on platters so that everyone can take individual portions onto their own plates. Of course, food can also be served separately in single portions as well, as is done in traditional Japanese cuisine. This entails quite a bit of effort gathering a supply of small plates, but the advantage is that you know exactly the amount in each individual serving. You can balance nutrition without worrying that something will be lacking.

I usually start setting my table in white and black. Many of my white dishes are unglazed porcelain, and I like their warm, handcrafted shape and crisp, glassy texture. I add black lacquered platters and chopsticks for contrast. Then, to this basic scheme, I add other items like earthenware, blue-and-white porcelain, carved wood, and glass.

Most Japanese tableware known overseas are expensive works of art or traditional crafts, but the country has a host of exciting new artisans creating new styles. Their works may not be as cheap as mass-produced factory ceramics, but they aren't outrageously expensive either. Japanese home cooking today is very much influenced by the West, and the same trends are taking place in Japanese design—modern tableware pieces look equally good in Western and Japanese dining rooms. I also sometimes use dishes of Western design, like the purple and pale pink vessels of the Italian artist Christiane Perrochon. Her works add flair and dynamism to the table while pairing excellently with Japanese cuisine.

One secret to buying good dishes is to avoid those with flat-looking, industrial colors in favor of those showing wonderfully uneven hues and individual textures. Try coordinating pieces of varying heights too, as this gives a sense of energy and movement to the table.

Beverages

Hot tea is, as you might expect, the most common drink accompanying a Japanese home meal. Aside from ordinary green tea, which many readers are probably familiar with, I often drink *hojicha*, a brown tea made of toasted leaves with a nutty aroma and a refreshing aftertaste. Iced barley tea is a summer favorite. As for alcohol, good choices to go with Japanese cooking include sake, as well as some white wines or dry sparkling wines. A light-bodied red wine can be excellent as well. If you've ever visited Japan, you will already know that we also love beer with our meals!

In a typical meal without alcohol, the rice, soup, and other dishes are served all at the same time. But if you'd like to focus first on enjoying drinking, you

can follow what is done in an *izakaya*, or Japanese pub: serve the side dishes first with the drinks, and then—when you've had your fill of alcohol—finish up with rice, miso soup, and perhaps some pickled vegetables. We often dine this way at home—in fact, making meals with my family, I think, is just as fun as going out to an *izakaya*!

Dessert

Japanese cooking uses very little butter or other dairy products, and so it follows that desserts are not very heavy either. In Japanese, dessert is sometimes referred to as *mizugashi*—a traditional term for "fruit"—and often as not, a few slices of fruit may be the only sweets offered after a meal. Or you might have refreshing jellies made of gelatin or agar, or sherbets and other ices. None of these sweets is rich in flour or butter, unlike Western desserts, and none is particularly fattening.

Notes

Mirin, a sweet wine, is often used in Japanese cooking, but is difficult to find abroad, so I suggest using maple syrup instead (preferably extra light). If, however, you do find *mirin*, be aware that it is not as sweet as maple syrup, so slightly more must be used to achieve the desired sweetness. (I would suggest that if a recipe in this book calls for 2 tablespoons maple syrup, then 2 ½ tablespoons *mirin* would be appropriate.) For a discussion of seasonings, oils, and other matters in the cooking process, please turn to the back pages.

In this book, one tablespoon equals 15 ml, one teaspoon 5 ml, and one cup approximately 240 ml. With my recipes, though, you generally don't need to be too strict about quantities. (In Australia, I know, a tablespoon equals 20 ml, and in my country, Japan, a cup equals 200 ml. For a detailed conversion chart, please see page 156.) But a rough measure will be quite sufficient. Think of the quantities as approximate targets that can be adjusted to your taste—a freedom that I believe should apply to cooking of any kind, anywhere in the world.

meat & poultry

Fried Chicken and Chive Rolls

I frequently made this dish when my daughters were young, for the *bento* lunch box they brought with them to their schools. It still tastes great even when cooled. My children have grown up, but I still make this for them when they visit me, with the only difference now being that they are served with a glass of red wine.

Serves four

1 boneless chicken thigh, skin-on (about 11 oz./310 g)
1 bunch chives
2 Tbsp maple syrup
2 ½ Tbsp soy sauce
2 Tbsp sake
½ cup cornstarch
½ cup water
Oil for deep-frying

1 Place the chicken thigh on a cutting board skin-side down and cut open the thicker part to make one large, flat piece. Lay the chives in a bundle on the chicken and roll tightly, securing with several toothpicks to prevent the roll from loosening (a).

a

2 Combine the maple syrup, soy sauce, and sake in a frying pan large enough to hold the chicken thigh, and bring to a gentle boil for 2 to 3 minutes.

3 Heat the oil for deep-frying to 340 to 350°F (170 to 180°C) in a heavy pot. *See detailed instructions on page 147.*

b

4 Combine the cornstarch with ½ cup water to make a stiff slurry (b). Pick up the chicken roll with tongs, place in the cornstarch mixture, and coat completely. Deep-fry in the oil until the surface crisps, for about 10 minutes. Remove the chicken from the oil and transfer to the sauce mixture in the frying pan. Roll the chicken in the sauce to coat completely.

5 Twist the toothpicks to loosen them and remove them from the chicken while hot. Cut the chicken rolls into ½-in. (1.5-cm) thick pieces and serve (a serrated knife works best for cutting the chicken).

NOTES

- Cornstarch can be substituted with potato starch (*katakuriko*) or tapioca powder.
- You'll know the exact consistency required of the starch mixture if you touch it. Though it might look a little dry and firm, it will immediately loosen when you scoop some up. The consistency is important because it ensures that just the right amount of starch adheres to the surface of the chicken, making the fried batter crispier, and able to absorb the sauce without becoming soggy.

Steamed Napa Cabbage and Pork Belly

Steaming is a great way to bring out the natural sweetness of vegetables. You don't need any special steaming equipment, only a pot large enough to hold the Napa cabbage, and a constant temperature inside the pot of about 212°F (100°C). As the cabbage wilts in the heat of the pan, it releases plenty of liquid that turns into steam, cooking the cabbage and pork. When you cut the cooked cabbage, use a tray with a rim to catch the mouthwatering juice and pour every drop into the serving bowl.

With the leaves still attached to the base of the Napa cabbage, slip the pork slices or smoked bacon at various intervals in between the leaves.

Serves four

¼ Napa cabbage
10 oz. (300 g) sliced fresh pork belly (or smoked bacon)
½ cup sake
1 Tbsp rice vinegar or white wine vinegar
Soy sauce and Japanese mustard for dipping

1 Without detaching the leaves from its base, wash the Napa cabbage quarter under cold running water, allowing the water to run between the leaves. Place upside down in a colander and allow to dry for a while.

2 Slip the pork belly slices or smoked bacon in between the leaves here and there. Gently shape the Napa cabbage back to its original form.

3 Set the Napa cabbage in a large pan, sprinkle with sake, and cover with a lid. Place over medium heat. When the cabbage begins to shed water, lower the heat to maintain a gentle simmer (the cabbage and pork will steam in their own juices). Continue to steam covered until the pork belly slices are just cooked, about 15 minutes. Sprinkle with the rice vinegar or white wine vinegar and remove from the heat.

4 Transfer the Napa cabbage onto a cutting board placed in a wide cooking tray with a rim to catch the juice. Cut into 1½-in. (3- to 4-cm) thick wedges and arrange in a serving dish with all of the juice. Serve with soy sauce and mustard for dipping.

NOTES

- Ask your butcher to get fresh pork belly and slice thinly.
- Japanese mustard is different from Dijon mustard. It doesn't contain vinegar and is a bit hotter. If it is not available, combine water and regular mustard powder to make a thick paste.

Fried Lotus Root Stuffed with Ground Chicken

Chanko hot pot, one of the staple meals of sumo wrestlers, is popular in Japan, and there are many *chanko* restaurants in downtown Tokyo. I ate this dish at one such restaurant a few years ago, and since it was so good, I tried to order more—but they refused outright! I decided to make the dish by myself. However, I was at a complete loss as to how to stuff the meat into the lotus holes, and must have stared at the ingredients for hours in my kitchen before coming up with an idea.

It was a little tricky to work out, but here's what you do. As you press the lotus root down into the ground chicken, the chicken will naturally fill the space in the holes. Don't season the ground chicken; salted meat will shed water while cooking and prevent the lotus root from becoming crispy. (It will have plenty of flavor with the soy sauce and mustard dip.) As the lotus root cooks, its texture becomes a little like a potato, but with a pleasant crispiness. I prefer to use unpeeled lotus root because I like the earthy flavor and aroma of the skin.

a

b

Serves four

5-in. (13-cm) length large lotus root
4 oz. (120 g) ground chicken
Oil for deep-frying
Soy sauce and Japanese mustard to taste

1 Wash the lotus root with its skin attached and blot dry. Cut off the ends. Heat the oil for deep-frying to 340°F (170°C) in a heavy pot.

2 Place the ground chicken on a small tray (a). Stuff the ground chicken into the holes in the lotus root by pressing and twisting the end of the lotus root down into the chicken (b). It may take some persistence. When the ground chicken fills the holes up to the top of the lotus root, cut the root into eight ½-in. (1.5-cm) thick pieces. Deep-fry until the pieces are golden brown.

3 Serve with the soy sauce and mustard for dipping.

NOTES

- I recommend using a large lotus root about 3 in. (8 cm) in diameter. The larger holes make stuffing easier.
- Ground pork can also be used.
- For more about Japanese mustard, see page 18.

Pan-roasted Duck Breast with *Mizuna* Greens

Mizuna is an herb-like leafy green, and is highly esteemed in Japan for its crisp, refreshing taste that perfectly offsets rich foods like duck breast. It is native to the old capital of Kyoto, but it is a mark of how far the popularity of Japanese cuisine has come that I have recently seen it growing in gardens in London.

With the faint mustardy tang of *mizuna* greens, rich duck meat becomes a satisfying healthy salad.

Serves four

1 bunch *mizuna* greens
14 oz. (400 g) duck breast
Salt and freshly ground black pepper
1 ½ tsp roasted sesame oil
3 Tbsp *ponzu* sauce
Freshly ground black pepper, or *yuzu-kosho* pepper paste to taste

1 Cut the *mizuna* greens into 2-in. (5-cm) lengths, soak in cold water to crisp and drain.

2 Pierce the fat side of the duck breast with a fork or score it by making shallow crosshatch cuts with a knife. Generously season the duck breast on both sides with salt and black pepper.

3 Heat a small frying pan over medium high heat (without any oil) until the heat is sufficient to make the duck breast sizzle when it touches the pan. Place the breast fat side down and sear for 5 minutes until most of the fat melts away and the skin becomes golden brown. Flip it over, cover the pan with a lid, turn the heat to low, and cook for another 5 minutes. Transfer to a cooling rack and let the meat rest for 7 minutes. Slice the duck breast thin at an angle.

4 Combine the roasted sesame oil, *ponzu* sauce, and black pepper (or the *yuzu-kosho* pepper paste) in a large bowl and toss with the duck breast slices and *mizuna* greens.

NOTES

▪ You can also use an oven to finish roasting. Transfer the duck breast to a baking dish after searing the fat side and roast for 8 minutes in a 450°F (230°C) oven.

Homemade *Ponzu* Sauce

Yields ⅔ cup

2 lemons, lime, or *yuzu* citrus, preferably unwaxed
4 Tbsp soy sauce
4 Tbsp *dashi* stock (*see* page 146)

Peel the lemon to get 1 tsp of zest. Squeeze the lemons and combine the juice with the zest, soy sauce, and *dashi* stock. For a more consistent flavor, measure the amount of lemon juice and add the same amount of soy sauce and *dashi* stock. *Ponzu* can be frozen in small amounts and used any time.

Beef Shabu-shabu with Thick Sesame Sauce

Shabu-shabu is originally a hot pot dish, and the name comes from the sound of swishing the beef slices in the pot. My version is like a meat salad, served at room temperature. The best part of this dish is savoring the texture of the soft sliced beef, but the meat will toughen if chilled or allowed to cool too long, so be sure to enjoy it soon after cooking.

Serves four

10 ½ oz. (300 g) paper-thin slices beef
4 florets broccoli, cooked in salted water
1 tsp ground sesame seeds

Thick Sesame Sauce:
- 2 Tbsp sesame paste
- 1 ½ Tbsp soy sauce
- 1 tsp sake

1 Combine all the ingredients of the Thick Sesame Sauce.

2 Bring a large pot of water to a boil. Swish the beef slices one by one (or in small batches) in the boiling water a few times until the color just changes from red to grey-brown, and transfer to a sieve to drain. Be careful not to overcook or the beef will become tough.

3 Dress the beef with the Thick Sesame Sauce and arrange in a serving bowl. If the sauce is too thick to dress the beef slices, loosen with a little water.

4 Serve with the florets of broccoli and top with the ground sesame seeds.

NOTES

- Ask your butcher to cut the tender part of beef chuck, rib, or loin into paper-thin slices. (Rib is the most expensive, but also the best for shabu-shabu.)
- It may take a long time, but you can cut a semi-frozen block of beef into shabu-shabu slices with a sharp knife. Be very careful as the semi-frozen meat makes the knife extremely slippery.

In Japan, well-marbled *wagyu* beef for shabu-shabu is cut using the ⅛-in. (3- to 4- mm) mark on the meat slicer.

Pork shoulder simmered over time makes it deliciously tender and easy to tear into shreds.

Simmered Pork Shoulder and Cabbage with Dijon Mustard

There are two main advantages to simmering pork shoulder. First, the meat becomes meltingly soft and pulls apart into tender shreds. Second, the excess fat is rendered out, mostly into the cooking liquid, and prevents the meat from drying out during the long cooking time. I love the combination of soy sauce and mustard as a sauce or dressing for meat dishes.

Serves four

14 oz. (400 g) boneless pork shoulder
2 tsp salt
¼ cabbage, cut into chunks
½ tsp salt
1 Tbsp Dijon mustard
2 Tbsp soy sauce

1. Bring a large pot of water to a boil and add 2 tsp salt. Add the pork shoulder and gently simmer for an hour. Lift it out onto a cutting board and pierce with a skewer. If pinkish liquid runs out, return the pork to the pot and cook a little further until the juices run clear. Let it cool in its cooking liquid until cool enough to handle.
2. Bring a medium pot of water to a boil and add ½ tsp salt. Add the cabbage and cook until softened but still crisp, then drain with a sieve. When cool enough to handle, squeeze out the remaining water.
3. Combine the Dijon mustard and soy sauce in a large bowl. Tear the pork shoulder into rough shreds by hand and add to the bowl along with the cabbage. Toss all the ingredients together.

NOTES

- In the UK, pork shoulder is sold as "pork shoulder," but in the US it is often divided into two parts: the "Boston butt" (upper pork shoulder) and the "picnic ham" (lower shoulder). I recommend using the Boston butt, which tends to have more flavor, but either works fine.

a

b

c

Simmered Pork Belly Cubes and Garlic

This is a local dish from Nagasaki, in the south of Japan, where my mother was born. She often simmered the pork belly cubes in this way until the pork rind would separate from the meat easily with chopsticks. This dish still evokes many happy memories of my mother.

It takes a long time to cook, but is not at all labor-intensive. Most of the fat is rendered out by the time it is done, but be sure to leave a little fat for flavor and that wonderful sensation of pork melting in your mouth. Fresh pork belly may be hard to find (most of it is turned into bacon), but it's worth asking your butcher if it's available.

Serves four to six

- 2 ¼ lbs. (1 kg) fresh pork belly
- 1 bulb garlic
- 3 cups sake
- 3 Tbsp sugar
- 3 Tbsp soy sauce
- Japanese mustard paste to taste

1 Cut the pork belly into 3 ½-in. (8-cm) cubes (a), (b). Separate the garlic cloves and peel. Place the pork cubes and garlic cloves in a large pot, pour in the sake, and add enough water to cover. Heat until barely simmering and cook over medium heat for 2 hours, skimming from time to time, until the pork cubes are soft. Add water when necessary to keep the pork barely covered.

2 Remove the pot from the heat and cool to room temperature. Transfer the pot to a refrigerator and chill overnight (or at least 8 hours).

3 Take the pot out of the refrigerator and remove most of the cold, coagulated fat (c). Bring to a boil over medium heat, add the sugar, and simmer for 20 minutes. Add the soy sauce and simmer for another 20 minutes.

4 Arrange in a serving bowl with a dab of Japanese mustard on the side.

NOTES

- 3 ¼-in. (8-cm) cubes may seem too large, but the pork belly will shrink by about two-thirds during simmering.

seafood

Marinated Tuna Salad

I was born in Japan, so I have been spoiled from childhood with the variety and quality of seafood that was always available. But high-quality tuna is one fish that can be easily found overseas. For this dish, it's not necessary to look for the expensive marbled, wild tuna belly. In fact, the brick-red dorsal section of regular farm-raised tuna, either fresh or frozen, is best. Extra-virgin olive oil wonderfully complements the lean, soft meat, and creates a smooth, silky texture on the tongue. Chives provide a contrast in aroma, texture, and color, but if you can find spring onions, sold in season at organic stores and farm markets, that's even better. Japan may have great seafood, but I'm always amazed at the availability of fresh (and inexpensive!) herbs in the West.

Serves four

10 oz. (300 g) sashimi-grade yellow fin tuna
¼ cup extra-virgin olive oil
1 to 2 Tbsp soy sauce
A handful of chives, cut into 2-in. (5-cm) lengths
2 cups lightly packed salad sprouts
2 tsp white sesame seeds, toasted
4 lime or lemon wedges

1 If the tuna is frozen, thaw overnight in the refrigerator wrapped in layers of paper towels, or soak overnight in cold salt water until thawed halfway. Place the tuna in a flat tray, pour over the olive oil and soy sauce, and dress well (a), (b). Cover and refrigerate for a half day or so, turning a couple of times.

2 Soak the chives and sprouts in ice water until crisp and drain well. Roast the sesame seeds in a small skillet over medium-low heat until they turn a light gold.

3 Cut the tuna into ¼-in. (6-mm) thick slices across the grain. In a medium bowl, combine the tuna, chives, sprouts, and sesame seeds. Check the taste and adjust the saltiness with soy sauce if needed.

4 Mound on a dish and serve with lime wedges.

NOTES

- Be sure to toast the sesame seeds to get that unique nutty aroma (pre-toasted sesame seeds just cannot compare). Use a heavy skillet, and shake it frequently, always adjusting the distance between the pan and flame. The sesame seeds first seem to sweat, releasing their oil and aroma, then begin popping slightly. If you continue just past the popping stage, you'll get golden sesame seeds with a deep, pervasive aroma. Toast them too long, however, and they'll burn, so be careful!

Salmon Teriyaki

Teriyaki is a salty-sweet dish enjoyed by all, young and old. My favorite teriyaki is made with fresh salmon, glazed with maple syrup, sake, and soy sauce.

Salmon Teriyaki

Mirin, a syrupy-sweet rice wine, is traditionally used for teriyaki, but I always substitute it with maple syrup when I'm outside Japan. It's easily available and because its boiling point is high, it prevents scorching while reducing the sauce. Once you master the ratio and method of making the teriyaki sauce, you can adjust the quantity and use it with all kinds of fish, such as sea bass and tuna. Of course, it's equally tasty with poultry and meats. Teriyaki is rich and salty-sweet, and needs something refreshing served on the side to clean the palate. I serve home-made *gari* ginger pickles (page 38), but bought in a store *gari* is fine. You can also serve grated daikon radish or fresh vegetables cut into thin needles.

Serves three to four

1 ½ lbs. (720 g) salmon fillet, skin-on, cut into 3 or 4 pieces
1 Tbsp olive oil
½ cup *gari* ginger pickles (*see* page 38)

Teriyaki mixture
⅓ cup sake
½ cup soy sauce
⅓ cup maple syrup or *mirin*

1 Carefully remove with tweezers any pin bones that may be in the salmon fillet (a), then cut it into 3 or 4 pieces.

2 In a small saucepan, bring the sake to a gentle simmer to evaporate the alcohol. Add the soy sauce and maple syrup and simmer for a few seconds. Transfer this teriyaki mixture into a flat tray (such as a baking dish), and let cool to room temperature. The salmon fillets can be marinated overnight in a refrigerator. If you do so, reserve 1 ½ cup of the mixture at this point in a separate bowl for later use in step 6.

3 Place the salmon fillets in the teriyaki mixture skin-side down and

leave for 10 minutes, basting from time to time (b). Flip the fillets over, skin-side up, and leave for another 10 minutes (c).

4 Preheat the oven to 390°F (200°C).

5 Heat a large frying pan on the stove top until hot. (Choose a pan that can be used in a hot oven, not one with a plastic or wooden handle, and avoid non-stick. Plain steel, cast iron, and stainless-steel-clad pans are all good choices.) Add the olive oil and swirl to coat the whole pan, then pour off the excess into a metal bowl. If any puddles of oil remain, carefully remove with paper towels. Return the pan to medium heat and lay the salmon fillets skin-side up (d). Transfer to the oven (e) and roast for 10 minutes until the insides of the fillets are just cooked. You don't need to flip the fillets. If the skin is not golden brown and crisp enough when the fillets are done, you can use the broiler in your oven to crisp the skin.

d

e

f

6 Remove the skillet from the oven and pour about 1 ½ cup of the teriyaki mixture over the fillets (f). Gently lift each fillet using a fish spatula and let the mixture run under the fillets. Carefully transfer the salmon fillets to a serving dish, skin-side up.

7 Bring the teriyaki mixture remaining in the frying pan to a gentle boil over low heat, and reduce for 3 to 4 minutes to thicken. Pour the sauce over the fillets and arrange the *gari* ginger pickles on the side.

NOTES

- It is very important to keep the skin on the salmon fillets to enjoy their crispness.
- Sesame or vegetable oil can be used instead of olive oil.
- The skillet will be very hot after removal from the oven, so please use thick oven mitts.

Gari Ginger Pickles

Most people have come across *gari* as a garnish for sushi, but it has many uses and is easily made at home. In Japan, there are many kinds of edible ginger, each with subtly different flavors, and all change color to a beautiful pale pink when pickled. *Shin shoga*, or new-crop ginger, is only available in early summer. It hasn't yet formed the tough, yellow fibers of mature ginger, and makes soft, smooth gari. *Oumi shoga*, produced near Kyoto, also has plump, juicy flesh. If you visit Japan in summer, you may find *yanaka shoga*, a small, tender ginger with leaves. And *ne shoga*, regular ginger, has tougher fibers. The ginger at some supermarkets, unfortunately, is old, and has dried out and become even tougher. If this is all you can find, slice it thinner and blanch it longer. On the other hand, pickles made from older ginger are refreshingly spicy, and go well with richer foods like grilled steak.

You can make variations of the basic recipe using other vinegars and other sweeteners. Enjoy experimenting with the ratio of the vinegar and sweetener to fit your taste.

4 oz. (120 g) fresh ginger
½ cup rice vinegar
¼ cup extra light maple syrup or *mirin*
½ tsp salt

1. Peel the ginger and thinly slice with the grain (a).
2. Combine the rice vinegar, maple syrup, and salt in a large bowl.
3. Bring a large pot of water to a boil and blanch the ginger for 50 seconds. If you can find tender new-crop ginger, blanch for only a few seconds (b). Remove the slices with a skimmer and drain for a few seconds, then immediately transfer to the bowl of pickling liquid. Let cool to room temperature (c).
4. The ginger pickles can be eaten soon after cooling, but they are tastier after a day or two in the refrigerator. They will keep about two to three months refrigerated in a clean container (d), (e).

Ginger is essential to Japanese cooking and comes in many varieties.

Vinegared Mackerel with Celery and Daikon Radish

I only make this salted and vinegared mackerel dish when I can find extraordinarily fresh mackerel. In Japan, fish is often combined with salt and vinegar, adjusting the amount of salt and vinegar and the marinating time depending on the fish and the season. I always make it on the strong side, so it goes well with vegetables.

I think that juicy, refreshing vegetables such as celery and daikon radish work great, with the dish becoming a salad where both fish and vegetables share the main role. If you don't feel comfortable eating marinated but uncooked mackerel, you can also grill it. In this case, slice the mackerel into slightly larger pieces, cut grooves into the skin, insert lemon or *yuzu* citrus slices, and grill over very high heat until the surface is just singed.

Serves six to eight

- 2 medium-sized mackerel fillets
- ½ cup salt
- 1 cup rice vinegar
- 1 stalk celery with leaves
- 3-inch (7.5-cm) thick cylinder of daikon radish
- 1 Tbsp grated ginger
- ¼ cup soy sauce

1 Remove the pin bones from the mackerel fillets with tweezers. Place the fillets on a wire rack over a flat tray (or anything that allows juices to drain from the fish). Generously sprinkle the mackerel on both sides with salt (a), cover, and refrigerate for an hour.

2 Blot the mackerel fillets dry with paper towels. Lay them skin-side down on a clean flat tray or in a baking dish deep enough for marinating. Pour the vinegar over the fillets until just covered. Marinate for 15 minutes for a lighter vinegar taste, or up to 30 minutes in the refrigerator for a stronger vinegar taste (b).

3 Peel the stringy fibers from the celery, cut into thin slices, and chop finely. Peel the cylinder of daikon radish and cut into thin slices. Soak each separately in ice water for a while to crisp and drain.

4 Remove the rib bones from the mackerel fillets with a knife. Gently remove the thin, transparent outer skin, starting from the head side and peeling towards the tail, leaving the black and silvery-blue inner skin still attached (c). Slice the fillets with a thin, sharp knife at a 45-degree angle, about ¼ in. (6 mm) thick. Remove any remaining pin bones as you cut. Arrange the slices on a platter, overlapping slightly. Top with the celery, celery leaves, and daikon radish, and serve the soy sauce and grated ginger on the side as a dipping sauce.

NOTES

- The mackerel must be absolutely fresh, with a plump, firm belly. The fattier the mackerel, the more salt should be used and the longer it should be marinated.

Wood-Grilled Fish with Grated Daikon Radish

I generally feel that charcoal grilling makes food taste better than gas or electric grilling, but ever since I started spending time abroad, I found that I prefer grilling over a wood fire. I love the different flavors created by wood and wood-chips, and the fact that wood-fired grilling can be a slow ritual enjoyed by the whole family.

Fish should be grilled skin-on to fully enjoy the smoky, juicy flavor and crispness. Grilled fish gives another great experience when served in the traditional Japanese style, with grated daikon radish to refresh the palate and soy sauce for extra seasoning.

Serves four

- 4 small-to-medium whole fish, skin-on, guts and gills removed
- A 3-inch (7.5-cm) thick cylinder of daikon radish
- Extra-virgin olive oil
- Sea salt
- Soy sauce

1 While the wood is still flaming, put the grill on to burn off any residue. Allow enough time for the wood to turn to embers, then smear the grill all over with paper towels soaked in olive oil.

2 Meanwhile, peel the daikon radish, grate, and drain in a fine-mesh sieve (a).

3 Lightly rinse the body cavity of the fish with salted cold water (made by combining 1 qt./1 L water with 2 Tbsp salt), and blot dry with paper towels (b). Rub 2 tsp olive oil over each fish (c), (d). Sprinkle evenly and liberally with sea salt (e).

4 Place the fish on the hot, oiled grill and grill both sides until the skin is partially blackened and crusted (f).

5 Arrange the fish on a serving dish along with the grated daikon radish. Diners then enjoy the fish by picking the skin and meat from the bones with chopsticks or a knife and fork, then mixing with a little grated daikon radish and soy sauce.

NOTES

- Some grills hold the embers on a raised platform, so you can grill food both under and over the embers. With one of these, you don't need to flip the fish, you can just move the grill with the fish on it under the embers to broil the topside.
- For this book I used black-throat perch. But rainbow trout, small snapper, sea bream, and small seabass or dover sole are all fine for grilling. (I love to grill sardines and herrings too.) Pacific saury (*samma*) or horse mackerel (*aji*) are superb grilled this way, if you can find them at your local Asian food store.

Carrot and *Tarako* Cod Roe

Carrots give dishes sweetness and a cheerful color, but eaten alone the flavor quickly becomes repetitive. This dish is meant to use a whole carrot, sautéing it to maximize its sweetness and adding a toasted flavor using the sesame oil. The *tarako* cod roe's popping, crunchy texture really makes the sautéed carrot come alive, and adds just the right saltiness and savoriness.

Serves four

1 carrot
1 sac (about 2 oz./60 g) *tarako* (salted cod or pollock roe)
2 tsp roasted sesame oil
2 tsp black or white sesame seeds

1 Peel the carrot and cut into thin slices at an angle. Stack the slices up in a small batch and flatten by displacing the layers a little, then cut into thin sticks from the side.

2 With the tip of a knife, make a shallow slit along the membrane covering the *tarako* sac. Squeeze the roe from the sac with the back of the knife, and discard the membrane.

3 In a medium saucepan heat the sesame oil over medium heat and cook the carrot, stirring often, until slightly softened. Add the *tarako* and cook, stirring constantly, until the roe turns white and becomes dry and separated. Add the sesame seeds and serve.

Remember to remove the membrane of the *tarako* cod roe.

NOTES

- Most Japanese or Korean grocery stores sell *tarako* (and some come with hot chili), either fresh or frozen in the seafood section. Usually one whole *tarako* has two sacs or lobes connected to each other at one end. This recipe calls for one sac or lobe.
- For a spicier taste, sprinkle with *shichimi*, Japanese seven-spice mix, when serving.
- Fresh or canned shad roe (a spring delicacy) can also be used, but you may want to add a little salt to the recipe.

Sautéed Squid in Butter and Soy Sauce

Before cooking squid (or shrimp)—whether grilling, steaming, or boiling—sprinkle it first with sake. The sake softens the squid flesh and encourages the coagulation of the proteins within, yielding a juicy and tender yet slightly crunchy texture. This technique also concentrates squid's natural *umami*; that elusive, savory flavor discovered in Japan but now appreciated everywhere. You can also enhance squid's *umami* by sautéing it until golden brown. Sautéing squid with butter and soy sauce (both full of *umami*) releases an extraordinary, dense flavor on the tongue. You may want to serve it with a wedge of lemon or lime, just to tone down the intensity.

a

b

Serves four

10 oz. (300 g) squid mantle, thawed if frozen
2 tsp sake or white wine
2 tsp olive oil
2 to 3 Tbsp unsalted butter
2 tsp soy sauce

1 Blot the squid mantles dry. Score the side with the thin, rough membrane in a crosshatch pattern at about ¼-in. (6-mm) intervals. Don't score straight up and down, but angle the knife about 45 degrees from vertical, so that the scoring will form a beautiful pinecone pattern as the squid is cooked (a), (b). Sprinkle the squid with the sake or white wine, cover, and let sit in the refrigerator overnight, or at least 8 hours.

2 Blot the squid dry again and cut into 1-in. (2.5-cm) pieces.

3 Pour the oil in a large frying pan over medium heat and wait until the surface begins to shimmer. Add the squid and sauté both sides until golden brown. Work in small batches so the pan doesn't get crowded. (If you obtain the squid with its tentacles still attached, sauté them separately with some extra olive oil after finishing the mantles.)

4 Stop the heat and remove the squid from the frying pan. Quickly wipe the pan, return to low heat, and add the butter. Return the squid to the pan, dress it with the melted butter, add soy sauce, and cook for 30 seconds.

NOTES

- Use your favorite squid, shrimp, or sea scallops for this dish. Calamari works well.

Miso-marinated Spanish Mackerel

Miso, a fermented paste of grains and soybeans, can be found easily in Asian markets or organic stores. I use ordinary yellow miso, but any variety will do as long as it is not too dark and salty. Be careful when grilling, because the sweet marinade chars easily. However, you will want *some* charred skin and blackened edges, to contrast with the sweet, juicy flesh on the inside. You may need to experiment with making this a few times, adjusting temperature and distance, to get used to your grill or broiler.

Serves four

Gauze or fine-mesh cheesecloth
11 oz. (310 g) Spanish mackerel, skin-on
4 stalks of broccoli rape
Salt

Marinade:
2 cups miso
½ cup maple syrup
(if you use sugar instead of maple syrup, combine ¼ cup sugar with ⅓ cup red wine and mix with the miso.)

1 Cut the fillet into four pieces. Lightly sprinkle with salt, place on a wire rack that fits in a tray, cover, and refrigerate overnight (or at least 8 hours) to drain excess water.

2 Blot the fillets dry with paper towels. Combine the miso and maple syrup in a bowl and mix well with a rubber spatula. The consistency of this marinade should be like mayonnaise. If the marinade is too thick, add a little of the sake or wine.

NOTES

- Purchase fish fillets with the skin on if possible, so they will not fall apart during marinating and grilling.
- Black cod, halibut, salmon, and scallops are also good for marinating in miso.

a

b

3 Use a flat-bottomed container with a lid large enough to fit the fillets. Spread half of the marinade evenly over the bottom of the container. Wrap the fillets with the gauze or cheesecloth in a single layer, place on the marinade (a), and cover completely with the remaining marinade. Cover the container and refrigerate overnight (at least 8 hours), or up to 3 days.

4 Heat the oven to 390°F (200°C) and cook the fillets skin-side up for about 12 minutes (b). You don't need to flip them. If the skin and edges are not yet golden brown, broil under high heat for a minute or so.

5 Blanch the broccoli rape in salted boiling water until soft but crisp, briefly shock in ice water, and drain. Lightly squeeze out the excess water by hand.

6 Arrange the fillets and broccoli rape on a serving dish.

Nori Seaweed and Mimolette Sandwiches

The briny flavor of *nori* seaweed and the aged, rustic flavor of Mimolette cheese make a surprisingly good combination. I was worried that these sandwiches would only appeal to people like me who grew up eating *nori*, but I've served them in Italy and my Italian friends love them. They look like elegant tea sandwiches, but they actually go better with white wine or sake.

Serves four

8 slices of Pullman bread (or any white sandwich bread)
4 sheets dried *nori* seaweed
(A standard *nori* sheet is 7 × 8 in./18.5 × 20.5 cm)
About $3\frac{1}{2}$ oz. (100 g) Mimolette cheese

a

b

1 Cut the crust off the Pullman slices and flatten with a rolling pin (a). Cut the cheese into $\frac{1}{8}$-in. (2- to 3-mm) thick slices (b). Cut the *nori* sheet into the same size as the flattened bread slices.

2 Lay the cheese slices on the bread, then top with a sheet of *nori* and another slice of bread. Wrap the sandwiches tightly with plastic wrap, press under a weight (a heavy baking dish with a flat bottom works well), and leave for 10 minutes.

3 Unwrap the sandwiches and cut into tea-style shapes with a long, sharp knife.

deep-frying

Shrimp and Scallop Cornmeal Tempura

In Japan, deep-frying does not have the unhealthy reputation it has in some parts of the West, and every home has a good deep-frying pot and a wire rack for draining. By following the techniques on page 147, you will be able to create tempura and other light, healthy fried foods. The tempura in this recipe uses cornmeal, which is not at all common in Japan. But while living abroad, I discovered cornbread and polenta, and fell in love with cornmeal. Deep-fried cornmeal releases a wonderful aroma and forms a light and extra-crispy batter. It also adds a delightful yellow color to the dish, a nice change from the standard shade of flour-based tempura. I like to serve with sea salt mixed with *matcha* (powdered green tea) to add a unique Japanese flavor, but plain sea salt tastes great as well.

Serves five

5 medium shrimp, still in the shell (with the heads on too, if possible)

3 large scallops

2 tsp flour

2 tsp water

5 *shiso* leaves or large basil leaves

1 sheet dried *nori* (A regular *nori* sheet is 7 × 8 in./ 18.5 × 20.5 cm), cut into 1-in. (2.5-cm) thick strips

1 cup cornmeal

1 egg white, beaten

Oil for deep-frying

1 tsp sea salt

1 tsp *matcha* powdered green tea

NOTES

▪ In supermarkets, there are often display cases with cooked shrimp and thawed, previously frozen shrimp, but you will get better quality buying frozen shrimp (with or without shells and head) than buying shrimp from a display case.

1 Thaw the shrimp if frozen and pat dry thoroughly with paper towels (a). Cut the tips off both the tails and the telsons (the spike just above the tail) with scissors (b). These parts contain water, and may burst and splash oil during frying. Leave the heads and tails on, but remove the shells from the body sections. Pick out the black vein with a toothpick. Cut the scallops into equal halves.

a

b

c

2 Combine the flour and water to make a slurry. Roll each shrimp with a *shiso* leaf (c), and stick the end of the leaf down with the slurry (d). Roll each scallop with a *nori* strip and also stick down with slurry.

3 Preheat the oil for deep-frying to 340°F (170°C) in a heavy pot. *See detailed instructions on page 147.*

4 Pour the cornmeal into a large bowl. Brush the shrimp and scallops with the beaten egg white, transfer into the bowl of cornmeal and coat lightly but evenly. Deep-fry the shrimp for about two minutes until they turn red and crispy. Deep-fry the scallops for two minutes until they turn light brown. Fry only 2 or 3 pieces at a time; then remove from the oil and place on a wire rack to drain.

5 Arrange the shrimp and scallops on a large plate and serve with a mixture of sea salt and *matcha* powdered green tea.

Kara-age Fried Chicken

Double-frying makes the surface of the chicken extra crispy. This soy-sauce marinated fried chicken is excellent with beer and wine, and one of my favorite dishes for entertaining at parties.

Kara-age Fried Chicken

Kara-age is a technique that uses potato starch as a coating that comes out especially crispy. I double-fry to ensure the chicken remains succulent and juicy, while retaining an extra-crispy coating. Deep-frying at a high temperature alone results in the chicken burned on the outside and still raw in the middle, but deep-frying first at a lower temperature, then again at a high temperature will guarantee a result that is both juicy and crispy as well as perfectly done. Deep-frying twice also helps when frying a large amount. You can pre-fry while waiting for your guests, then finish frying at just the right moment to serve the hot, crispy chicken.

Serves six to eight

1 whole chicken

Marinade
- ½ cup soy sauce
- ¼ cup sake
- 1 knob ginger, cut into slices
- 2 to 3 scallions, cut into chunks
- 2 to 3 cloves garlic, cut into slices

⅔ cup potato starch or cornstarch
⅓ cup water
3 Tbsp flour
Oil for deep-frying
Lemon wedges to taste

1 Combine all the ingredients of the marinade in a large bowl. Cut the bone-in chicken into bite-size pieces with a cleaver (or have your butcher do it). Add the chicken to the marinade (a) and leave in a refrigerator for at least 2 hours.

2 Preheat the oil for deep-frying to 340°F (170°C) in a heavy pot. *See detailed instructions on page 147.*

a

b

c

d

e

f

g

h

NOTES

- If you buy chicken in pieces, try to have a good mix of thighs, breast, wings, and legs.

3 Transfer the marinated chicken pieces into a sieve to drain. Make a slurry with potato starch (or cornstarch) and water in a bowl (b). *See page 147 for the details of consistency.*

4 Dust the chicken with flour and pat off any excess. Roll the pieces in the slurry (c), (d), then gently slip them into the hot oil (e) and deep-fry until lightly colored, about 15 minutes. The oil may splatter, so it is a good idea to use a deep-frying screen if available (f). As the chicken pieces are fried, transfer onto a wire rack to drain.

5 Heat the same oil, this time to 370°F (190°C). In small batches, deep-fry the chicken pieces again until golden brown, about 2 to 3 minutes. As they are fried, remove from the oil and place on a wire rack to drain.

6 Arrange the chicken pieces on a plate and serve with lemon wedges.

Kaki-age Fried Corn and Shrimp

Kaki-age is a frying technique that creates a small sphere or disc of mixed ingredients held loosely together with crispy tempura batter. When Japanese make tempura at home, they might include *kaki-age* made from a mix of seasonal ingredients alongside the regular items such as shrimp and sweet potato. New crop carrot and onions in spring, corn and *edamame* beans in summer, a variety of mushrooms in autumn, and shredded *gobo* burdock root and onions in winter; there are infinite variations. Sliced squid, shrimp, and scallops can be mixed in with the vegetables, adding a sweet, satisfying seafood flavor.

Serves four

1 ear fresh corn, husk removed
4 large shrimp, thawed if frozen
1 egg, beaten
⅓ cup all-purpose flour or plain flour
Oil for deep-frying
Sea salt

1 Preheat the oil for deep-frying to 340°F (170°C) in a heavy pot. *See detailed instructions on page 147.*

2 Cut the kernels off the corn. Pat the shrimp thoroughly dry with paper towels and cut into ½-in. (1-cm) pieces. Put the corn kernels and shrimp pieces in a large bowl (a), then add the flour and mix. Add the beaten egg and mix just a few times; lumps are acceptable (b). The batter should be just thick enough to hold the corn and shrimp together.

a

b

c

d

3 Scoop up the mixture with a large dinner spoon and gently slip into the hot oil (c). Use another spoon to hold it together if needed. Deep-fry until golden, about 4 to 5 minutes (d). Remove from the oil and place onto a wire rack to drain (e). Repeat until the mixture is gone, creating at least four pieces.

4 Arrange on a dish and sprinkle with the sea salt (f).

e

f

Su-age Fried *Kabocha* Pumpkin

Su-age is a frying technique that uses no batter or coating of any kind. *Kabocha* pumpkin has a deep-green edible skin and bright orange to yellow flesh. If you are unable to find *kabocha*, substitute regular pumpkin or acorn squash, but you will need to peel them. In any case, garnish with fresh ginger sticks, since ginger and pumpkin go so well together.

Kabocha releases a sweet aroma when cooked and its texture becomes surprisingly smooth.

Serves four

1 lb. plus 2 oz. (about 500 g) *kabocha* pumpkin

Oil for deep-frying

1 large knob ginger

Soy-maple *dashi* sauce:

- 1 Tbsp maple syrup or 3 Tbsp *mirin*
- ¼ cup soy sauce
- 1 cup *dashi* stock (*see* page 146)

1 Cut the *kabocha* in half (if it is whole), remove the seeds, and cut into ¾-in. (1.5- to 2-cm) thick wedges. (See the note below.)

2 Combine all the ingredients of the soy-maple *dashi* sauce in a large saucepan over low heat and keep warm.

3 Heat the oil for deep-frying to 325°F (160°C) in a heavy pot. *See detailed instructions on page 147.*

4 Deep-fry the *kabocha* wedges until slightly softened. Increase the oil temperature to 350°F (180°C) and continue to deep-fry until the surface of the pumpkin becomes a little crispy. Remove from the oil and place on a wire rack to drain.

5 While still hot, slip the *kabocha* wedges into the saucepan of soy-maple *dashi* sauce. Peel the ginger, and cut into slivers.

6 Arrange in a serving bowl and top with the thin ginger sticks.

NOTES

- Raw *kabocha* squash can be very hard, so please be careful when cutting. I use a heavy Chinese cleaver, using my left hand to press down on the back of the knife. If the *kabocha* is too hard, microwave it a little to soften it.

Taro and Shrimp Quenelles

Taro is a starchy, potato-like tuber. It can be served by itself, steamed, or simmered, but it really shines as a binder for other ingredients. Unlike flour or pure starches like cornstarch, taro adds a deep, earthy flavor and a complex, interesting texture. I always fry a large batch of these quenelles and freeze the extras. The leftovers make a wonderful soup with *dashi* stock and a few vegetables.

When mixing in a food processor, try to retain some of the texture of the shrimp and taro roots.

Serves four

8 large shrimp, thawed if frozen
5 small to medium knobs taro root
½ tsp salt
Oil for deep-frying
1 tsp *matcha* powdered green tea
½ tsp sea salt

1 Preheat the oil for deep-frying to 340°F (170°C) in a heavy pot. *See detailed instructions on page 147.*

2 Pat the shrimp thoroughly dry with paper towels. Rinse any dirt off the taro root and peel with a knife.

3 Put the taro roots in a food processor and pulse 10 to 12 times until they are broken down into rough pieces. Add the shrimp and salt and pulse 4 to 5 times more. Transfer the mixture into a bowl, scraping out the food processor with a rubber spatula.

4 Make quenelles using two large dinner spoons and drop each quenelle into the hot oil. Deep-fry until golden brown, remove from the oil, and place onto a wire rack to drain.

5 Arrange on a serving plate along with a mound of *matcha* powdered green tea mixed with sea salt.

vegetables

Grand Vegetable Platter with Onion Vinegar Dressing

There's something quite luxurious about a large assortment of vegetables so check your markets for exceptional ingredients at the peak of their season, and take care to cook the vegetables just right in order to highlight their individual texture and aroma. I believe a platter like this one that is prepared with warmth and sincerity catches people's attention and expresses heartfelt hospitality to friends and family. Don't be constrained by the list below. Use fresh celery and radicchio, steamed or roasted summer sweet corn, cooked winter greens such as mustard greens or swiss chard, potatoes and zucchini for deep-frying; anything that is in season. The versatile yet tasty Onion Vinegar Dressing will pull them all together.

Blanch the greens while retaining their crispness.

Serves four

These are just examples, use any vegetables you have:

Raw: *Mizuna* greens, salad onions, watercress, tomatoes

For blanching: Sugar snap peas, green beans

For deep-frying in olive oil: Parsnips, *kabocha* pumpkin, carrots, shiitake mushrooms

Onion Vinegar Dressing (*see* page 70)

1 For raw vegetables: crisp the greens by soaking in ice-cold water and draining well in a sieve. If you are blanching and frying other vegetables, set the sieve over a bowl and put in a refrigerator to keep fresh. Onions usually have a bitter, harsh taste when eaten raw, so slice them thinly, soak in cold water for about 20 minutes, then wrap with a cheesecloth, paper towels, or *sarashi* (Japanese cotton cloth) and squeeze out the water. Separate the onion slices before use.

2 For blanched vegetables: peel the tough strings off the sugar snap peas, then blanch in salted boiling water until tender but still crunchy. Do the same for the green beans.

3 For deep-fried vegetables: peel the carrots and parsnips (or leave the peels on for an earthier flavor) and cut into bite-size pieces. Deep-fry the vegetables without any batter in 350°F (180°C) olive oil until tender. *For preparing kabocha pumpkin, see details on page 62.*

4 Arrange all the vegetables on a large platter and serve with the Onion Vinegar Dressing.

Vegetables served raw should be soaked in ice-cold water to remain crisp and chilled.

Onion Vinegar Dressing

This dressing makes any vegetable delicious and easy to eat, and the flavor will change depending on the strength of the onion. You can substitute the standard onion with a sweet variety, like Vidalia, Wala Wala, Granex, or Supasweet onion. But don't worry—even if the onion dressing has a harsh taste, it will mild up in a couple of days. The dressing should be emulsified until thick, looser than mayonnaise but thicker than vinaigrette. It works well as a dip or as a marinade. I also love it as a sauce for meat or fish that is grilled until well-browned.

Makes 1½ cups

- ½ onion
- ½ cup rice vinegar
- 1 cup olive oil
- 1 heaping tsp salt
- 1 tsp black peppercorns

Remove the stem ends of the onion (a) and cut into chunks (b). Put all the ingredients in a tall, round, cylinderical container, such as a jam jar, not one made of aluminum (c). Insert a stick blender all the way to the bottom and mix until emulsified (d). If you don't have access to a stick blender you can mix in a stand blender or food processor and then pour into a jam jar. Keep in the refrigerator for up to a week.

bamix
la base

Mushrooms in *Kombu* Broth with Citrus

Vegans especially will love this flavorful and nutritious dish. There is no rule for selecting the types of mushrooms: choose from shiitake, *maitake*, oyster, button, *eryngi* (also called French horn mushrooms), *shimeji*, and others. The larger the variety, the better this dish will be. I also like to try unfamiliar mushrooms I find at the market for this recipe.

Bright, yellow *yuzu* can be seen everywhere during winter in Japan. They are about the same size as a baseball.

Serves four to six

1 piece dried *kombu* kelp, 2 × 4 in. (5 × 10 cm)
Various mushrooms, enough to fill about 3 ½ qt. (3.5 L) pot
2 tsp soy sauce
1 Tbsp sake
1 tsp salt
Lemon peel or *yuzu* citrus peel, white pith removed, and cut into slivers

1 Fill a 3 ½ qt. (3.5 L) pot half-full with water and add the *kombu*. Leave in the refrigerator overnight (or at least 8 hours), or let stand for at least 3 hours.

2 Remove the hard part of the stalks from the mushrooms and wipe off any dirt. If large, tear by hand into bite-size pieces.

3 Add the mushrooms to the pot of *kombu* kelp and water, and then add the soy sauce, sake, and salt. Stir from the bottom a few times. Cover the pot with a lid. Bring to a gentle simmer and cook for 10 minutes over medium heat until the mushrooms shrink and the water becomes flavored with the mushrooms and *kombu* kelp.

4 Lay the *kombu* in the bottom of a large serving bowl, ladle in the mushrooms, pour in the soup, and top with the citrus shreds.

Mushrooms, when boiled, release an array of flavors to make a mouthwatering soup.

NOTES

- *Kombu* soup gives this dish a quintessentially Japanese flavor, but of course you can use chicken stock instead. This is a hearty, comfort soup; perfect for those chilly, winter days.

Lemon-scented Celery, Daikon Radish, and Crab

Daikon radish can be meltingly soft when cooked in soup, but is crisp and juicy when eaten raw. This refreshing salad combines the juicy crispness of the raw daikon radish and celery, the sweet richness of crab, and a touch of citrus. After too much dining out, this salad will rest and reset your taste buds.

The ubiquitous daikon radish has an array of textures in Japanese cuisine.

Serves four

5 oz. (140 g) cooked, frozen king crab legs in shell
1 celery stalk
1 cylinder daikon radish, about 2-in. (5-cm) long
2 tsp sea salt
1 lemon or ½ *yuzu* citrus

1 Completely thaw the crab legs in a refrigerator overnight. Cut open the shells with shears and remove the meat, discarding the shells and cartilage.

2 Remove the tough strings from the celery stalk and cut into 2.5-in. (5-cm) lengths. Cut the thicker parts of the celery stalk into halves or thirds to make the pieces about the same size. Peel the daikon radish and cut into pieces about the same size as the celery. Combine the celery and daikon radish in a bowl and sprinkle with the salt. Transfer to a colander or strainer and let stand to drain.

3 Grate the lemon skin to make one heaping Tbsp of zest. Squeeze the lemon to make about 2 Tbsp of juice.

4 Combine the celery, daikon radish, and crab meat in a bowl and toss with the lemon juice. Let stand for 10 minutes for the flavors to combine. Arrange in a serving bowl and top with a mound of lemon zest.

Steamed Taro with Maple-miso Dip

You must find small taro roots, not the large, purplish Hawaiian kind, for this recipe. They are best eaten by squeezing the skin until the flesh pops out, still attached to its skin, then dipping it into the maple-miso dip, and nibbling the flesh off the skin. They make a great snack and a good alternative to potato chips or French fries.

Serves four

20 small to medium taro roots
3 Tbsp yellow miso
1 ½ Tbsp maple syrup

1 Rinse any dirt off the taro roots in cold water, drain, and score a cross on the bottom of each one with a paring knife. Steam or microwave about 20 minutes, or until tender when pierced with a skewer.

2 Mix the miso and maple syrup together in a small bowl.

3 Serve the steamed taro root with the maple-miso dip.

Taro root is easily popped out of its skin when cooked.

Crunchy Vegetable Batons with Roasted Sesame Oil Dressing

Roasted sesame oil combined with ginger and scallion has a pleasant Chinese character. It tastes good with many vegetables, so try it with anything in season that can be cut into crunchy batons. However, you should always include the deep-fried eggplant, whose juicy and tender texture plays a counterpoint to the other vegetables.

Serves four

Roasted Sesame Oil Dressing (Makes ½ cup)

- 4 Tbsp soy sauce
- 2 Tbsp rice vinegar
- 1 ½ Tbsp roasted sesame oil
- 2 Tbsp finely chopped scallion, preferably white part only
- 1 small knob ginger, finely chopped

2 Japanese cucumbers or ½ English cucumber
1 stalk celery
8 to 10 green beans
Salt
3 small Japanese or Italian eggplants
Oil for deep-frying

1 Combine all the ingredients for the dressing in a small bowl. Set aside.

2 Peel the Japanese or English cucumber, leaving some green skin still attached, cut into 2-in. (5-cm) lengths, then cut into 4 equal wedges. For the larger English cucumber, cut into six or eight equal wedges.

3 Remove the tough strings from the celery stalk and cut into 2-in. (5-cm) lengths. If it is thick, cut into half lengthwise.

4 Blanch the green beans in salted boiling water and drain in a sieve. When cool enough to handle, cut into 2-in. (5-cm) lengths.

5 Trim the eggplants, cut into halves crosswise, then cut into 8 equal wedges. Deep-fry in 360°F (180°C) oil until tender, 5 to 7 minutes.

6 Arrange the vegetables on a serving plate along with a bowl of dressing. Serve not by dipping but by arranging the batons on individual plates and pouring the dressing over the top.

When chopping the scallion, first cut along the fibers, then across.

Goya-champlu Stir-fried Bitter Squash

The bumpy, oblong *goya* is a bitter squash around 1 ½ in. (4 cm) in diameter and 8 in. (20 cm) long. It is popular in China and Vietnam, and recently in Japan, especially in Okinawa, where people live longer than even most other Japanese. It is full of vitamin C and taurine, which is good for high-blood pressure. Its bitterness becomes addictive during the heat of summer.

Although bitter, *goya* is widely enjoyed across Asia, where it is recognized for its health benefits.

Serves four

1 bitter squash
Salt
2 tsp roasted sesame oil
2 eggs, beaten
1 tsp soy sauce
½ cup bonito shreds, plus extra for topping

1. Cut the bitter squash in half lengthwise and scrape out the seeds and pith (the fluffy white part is bitterest) using a spoon. Cut each half into ¼-in. (6-mm) thick slices. Put the slices in a colander and sprinkle generously with salt, then toss to distribute the salt evenly, and set over a bowl. Leave for 10 to 15 minutes to drain, then pat thoroughly dry with paper towels.
2. Heat the roasted sesame oil in a frying pan over medium-high heat and cook the bitter squash slices until softened but still crunchy, about 2 to 3 minutes. Add the beaten eggs and briefly stir-fry until the eggs are loosely coagulated. Immediately add the soy sauce and the dried bonito shreds and remove from the heat.
3. Arrange on a serving dish and top with a mound of dried bonito shreds.

tofu

Homemade Tofu

EQUIPMENT

To make tofu, some special equipment is required. First, a deep pot, such as a pasta pot or stockpot, is needed. The blended soybean mixture will foam up to almost double in volume when heated, so the rim of the pot should be at least twice as high as the level of the mixture. I use a pot 8 in. (20 cm) deep and $9\frac{2}{3}$ in. (24 cm) in diameter.

You also need a *sarashi*, a Japanese plain cotton cloth, at least 14 × 28 in. (34 × 70 cm) large, to strain the hot soybean mixture. Gauze or fine-mesh cheesecloth can be substituted. A wire mesh-type collander (page 134) that fits neatly into a bowl is best for straining the soy milk, though a perforated colander will also work. I use a bowl-shaped strainer and a bowl about $8\frac{1}{2}$ in. (21 cm) deep and $3\frac{2}{3}$ in. (9 cm) in diameter.

You need thick rubber gloves to avoid scalding your hands when pressing (or you can wait until the mixture cools a little). I use the same strainer and *sarashi* cloth for draining the curds, so the shape naturally comes out round. If you have a special wooden tofu mold, or fine-mesh bamboo sieve, you can make authentic-looking blocks and rounds of tofu. You will also need a thermometer, blender, medium-size pot for heating the strained soymilk, a ladle, and a wooden spatula.

Makes about 12 oz. (350 g) tofu

$10\frac{1}{2}$ oz. (300 g) dried soybeans
About 1 Tbsp *nigari* coagulant
(Check the package for the right amount and usage)

1 Soak the soybeans in plenty of water and leave in the refrigerator overnight (or at least 8 hours) (a). The beans should be plump and fully rehydrated (b). Discard any odd-shaped or colored beans.

2 Separate the beans from the liquid in which they've been soaking. Place some of the beans in a blender and pour in the liquid until it comes to about 1 in. (2.5 cm) above the beans (c). Blend until smooth and creamy (d), first at low speed, and then higher speed. Work in small batches, filling no more than half the capacity of the blender. If you run out of the liquid, use water.

3 Place the mesh colander over anything that will catch the strained soy milk, such as a medium-sized pot just smaller than the colander. Dampen the *sarashi* cloth with water, wring it out as thoroughly as possible, and lay over the mesh bowl. Set aside (e).

4 Pour the soybean mixture into a deep pot up to half the depth of the pan. Cook over medium heat, always scraping the bottom of the pan with a wooden spatula to prevent sticking and scorching. Watch the pot closely: as the mixture is heated, the volume increases quickly (f). Just before it boils over, remove the pan from the heat and wait until the foam subsides. Cook again over very low heat for 10 minutes, scraping the bottom with the spatula (g).

5 Pour the hot mixture into the bowl prepared in step 3 (h). Gather up the edges of the cloth and twist, pressing down to squeeze out the soy milk (i), (j). Rubber gloves may be required if it is very hot. The pulp left in the *sarashi* is called *okara* (k), and is very good for you (it's very good sautéed with garlic and vegetables).

6 Pour the soymilk into a regular pot and cook over medium heat, stirring with a spatula to keep an even temperature throughout (l). When the temperature reaches 170 to 175°F (75 to 80°C), remove the pot from the heat, pour in the *nigari* coagulant, and stir three times very, very gently (m). Cover the pot and let it sit undisturbed for 15 minutes.

e

f

g

h

i

j

k

l

m

7 Meanwhile, wash the *sarashi* cloth with water and wring it out thoroughly. Place the mesh colander in the bowl and spread the *sarashi* over the top.

8 Scoop up the tofu curd from the pot and pour into the *sarashi* in the bowl (n). Discard any cloudy liquid that drains into the bowl (o). Leave the curd for 30 minutes to allow it to set.

9 Soak the finished tofu in ice water for an hour to remove some of the *nigari* coagulant (p).

n

o

p

NOTES

■ You can leave the tofu mixture to sit longer in step 6. The curd will coagulate in the pot into a tender, fragile-textured tofu, called *oboro-dofu*. If you scoop out servings of *oboro-dofu* with a ladle, it is called *kumiage-dofu*, meaning "scooped-out" tofu. If the curd is scooped into a container, it is called *yose-dofu*. When the curd is placed in a fine-mesh bamboo sieve and drained only by the weight of the tofu itself, it is called *zaru-dofu*, which means "sieve" tofu. All these variations contain more water than regular *momen-dofu*, and are more tender and smoother in texture. *Kinugoshi-dofu* or *kinu-dofu* is silky-smooth tofu that requires professional equipment and artisanal technique.

Yakumi-dofu

Yakumi-dofu is a simple way of enjoying tofu, with a few fragnant garnishes (chopped scallions, grated ginger, and young *shiso* buds), and shreds of dried bonito and soy sauce for seasoning. *Shichimi* seven-spice mix can be served on the side. *Yakumi-dofu* is often chilled, but I love to eat it when the tofu has only cooled to room temperature, which maximizes the sweet flavor of the soy milk.

Deep-fried Tofu in *Dashi* and Soy Sauce

Serves four to six

1 block homemade or soft tofu, 12 oz. (340 g)

Soy-maple *dashi* sauce:

- 1 Tbsp maple syrup or 3 Tbsp *mirin*
- 1/4 cup soy sauce
- 1 cup *dashi* stock (*see* page 146)

Oil for deep-frying

1/2 cup flour (use weak flour, such as pastry or cake flour, for a crisper texture)

2 Tbsp finely chopped scallion

2 Tbsp grated ginger

4 *shiso* leaves, shredded (optional)

Slices of fresh red chili pepper (optional)

1 Leave the tofu on the tray to drain for about 10 minutes, until it becomes a little firmer (a). Cut into 2-in. (5-cm) cubes.

2 Combine all the ingredients of the soy-maple *dashi* sauce in a small saucepan over low heat and keep warm.

3 Heat the oil to 375°F (190°C) in a heavy pot. Dust the tofu cubes with the flour (b), and pat off any excess. Deep-fry the tofu cubes until the surface is light gold, and drain on a wire rack for a minute or two. Then re-fry the cubes in 375°F (190°C) oil until the surface is golden and crisp.

4 Arrange the tofu in a serving bowl and pour over the sauce. Top with the chopped scallion, grated ginger, shredded *shiso*, and red chili pepper slices to taste.

Sautéed Tofu with Ginger

Serves four

- ½ block homemade or soft tofu, 6 oz. (170 g)
- 1 knob ginger, finely chopped
- 2 tsp roasted sesame oil
- ¼ carrot, peeled and cut into thin sticks
- 2 green beans, cut into thin slices at an angle
- 1 tsp soy sauce
- 1 Tbsp dried *hijiki* seaweed (optional)

NOTES

- Instead of tofu, *okara*, a by-product of tofu, works just as well for this recipe (*see* page 83).

1 Wrap the tofu in plenty of paper towels or *sarashi* cloth, and rest a plate or small wooden tray on top to even out its shape and allow it to drain for about 30 minutes, or use ready-made firm tofu.

2 If using the *hijiki* seaweed, soak in plenty of water for 30 minutes (check the package for the correct soaking time) and drain in a sieve. Cut into bite-size lengths.

3 Put the roasted sesame oil and chopped ginger in a medium frying pan (preferably a Teflon coated non-stick pan) over low heat until the ginger releases its flavor. Add the carrots and green beans and sauté until soft. Add the *hijiki* and sauté to evaporate most of its water. Add the tofu, crumbling by hand into large lumps. With a flat spatula or fish spatula mix all the ingredients by turning the lumps of tofu over in the pan (don't worry if the tofu crumbles further), until the tofu is heated through. Add the soy sauce, turn a few more times, and remove from heat.

Make sure the weight of the plate is not too heavy, or you will squash the tofu.

福

traditional specialties

Yakitori Grilled Chicken, Yoko Style

Yakitori, literally "grilled chicken," is a Japanese favorite—small chicken pieces skewered onto bamboo sticks and grilled over charcoal. Most people are picky about where the chicken was raised and many people have favorite parts (including the organs), so there are many varieties of *yakitori* stands and restaurants in Japan.

When I'm away from Japan, I sometimes miss the aroma of grilled *yakitori* and sweet teriyaki sauce, so I make it myself when abroad. But if I grill chicken on a gas range, it's hard to air out the kitchen—the grilled aroma tends to hang around. So I cook the chicken pieces in the oven and dress with a kind of teriyaki sauce. Most *yakitori* is boneless, but this way I can cut up a whole chicken and broil it bone-in, which is tastier and more fun to eat. I also like broiling plenty of vegetables to go along with the chicken.

Serves four

1 chicken, about 3 lbs. (1 to 1.5 kg)
2 leeks, white part only
12 sweet chili peppers, such as Anaheim or Romano peppers

Yakitori sauce:
- 1/3 cup sake
- 1/4 to 1/3 cup maple syrup
- 2/3 cup soy sauce

Sansho pepper powder or *shichimi* spice powder (optional)

1 Preheat oven to 410°F (210°C).

2 For the sauce: Put the sake in a large saucepan over low heat and bring to a simmer to evaporate the alcohol. Add the maple syrup and soy sauce and return to a gentle simmer. Cook until the liquid is slightly reduced and thickened.

3 Remove any excess fat from the chicken and cut into chunks using a Chinese cleaver. Cut the leeks into 2-in. (5-cm) pieces.

4 Line an oven tray with parchment paper and lay the chicken pieces skin-side up. Roast in the oven for about 20 minutes until the skin becomes golden brown, then turn over with tongs (a). Return to the oven and roast 5 to 7 minutes more. Immediately transfer the chicken into the saucepan and dress well.

5 Broil the leeks and chili peppers in a broiler, turning over until browned in places. Transfer to the pan of chicken and sauce and dress well.

6 Transfer the chicken, leeks, and chili peppers to a large bowl (c). Bring the remaining sauce to a gentle simmer, and cook 1 to 2 minutes to thicken further.

7. Arrange the chicken, leeks, and chili peppers in a serving bowl. Spoon the sauce over the chicken and sprinkle with *sansho* pepper or *shichimi* spice powder, if desired.

NOTES

- Instead of leeks and chili peppers, use whatever vegetables you have that are good when grilled. Onion, broccoli, bell peppers, asparagus, and zucchini are all delicious.

Homemade *Shiozake* Salted Salmon

In Japan, salted salmon fillets are packed and sold for grilling at home. But the fillets are actually easy to prepare from scratch, and because great fresh salmon can be found abroad, I often make it myself. It is important to use fine-grain sea salt. I also suggest asking your fishmonger to include the belly of fresh salmon. My favorite way to eat grilled, salted salmon belly is to put it in a bowl of hot white rice and pour *hoji-cha,* a fragrant tea made from toasted green tea leaves, over the top.

For salting the salmon evenly, rub a liberal amount of fine-grain sea salt all over.

Serves four

1 ⅓ lb. (600 g) fresh salmon fillet, skin-on
¼ cup fine sea salt

1 Place a wire rack on a tray with a rim to catch drips, and lay the salmon fillet on the rack skin-side up. Generously rub the sea salt all over. Put a single layer of plastic wrap on the salmon fillet and put about 3 ⅓ lbs. (1.5 kg) of weight on the salmon. (I use 3 stainless-steel small trays that weigh the right amount). Refrigerate overnight (or 8 hours), or up to 4 days.

2 Preheat oven to 390°F (200°C). Blot dry the salmon fillet with paper towels and cut into large pieces. Place on a wire rack skin-side up and roast for 10 minutes, without flipping. If the skin is not crispy and browned, put under a broiler until the skin becomes crisp.

NOTES

- Ask your fishmonger to leave the skin on. If possible, purchase salmon with the belly intact, which tastes especially good salt-dried and roasted.

Namban-zuke Fried Fish in Sweet-and-sour Marinade

Namban-zuke is one of the dishes that many foreigners traveling in Japan come to love. Back home, of course, horse mackerel may be difficult to find, but the *namban-zuke* marinade tastes good with any oily fish, and also with bone-in chicken pieces. *Dashi* stock is required for the recipe, but feel free to use instant *dashi* powder. The key to the recipe is to slow-fry, especially when using small whole fish. If you slow-fry the fish and marinate for 1 or 2 days, the bones become tender enough to eat, and are a good source of calcium. This is so good, though, you'll have to resist eating it all the first day of marinating!

Use any variety of hot pepper for this dish.

Serves four

Sweet-and-sour Marinade:

- ½ cup *dashi* stock (*see* page 146)
- ½ cup rice vinegar
- ½ cup soy sauce
- 2 to 3 Tbsp maple syrup

12 *aji* (horse mackerel), each 4 in. (10 cm) long, cleaned

½ cup flour

Olive oil for deep-frying

1 red onion, sliced

2 hot chili peppers, fresh or dried, sliced at an angle

1 Combine all the Sweet-and-sour Marinade ingredients in a small saucepan. Bring to a simmer and stop the heat. Transfer to a large bowl and cool to room temperature.

2 Heat the oil for deep-frying to 340°F (170°C) in a heavy pot. Dust the horse mackerel with the flour and pat off any excess. Dip each horse mackerel in the hot oil head down, holding the tail for a few seconds before releasing the fish. The temperature of the oil will drop, so adjust the heat from time to time. Once all the fish have been added, fry for ten minutes, or until the bubbles become small and the surface of the fish looks dry and crisp.

3 Transfer the fish into the bowl of marinade. Add the red onion and red chili peppers to the bowl and let marinate for at least 30 minutes. The fish can be marinated up to 2 days in the refrigerator.

NOTES

- Instead of horse mackerel, try fresh sardines, salmon, or mackerel fillets—even chicken pieces are great fried and marinated in sweet vinegar.
- *Dashi* stock can be substituted with sake. In this case, simmer about ⅔ cup of sake in a small saucepan for 1 minute to evaporate the alcohol.

Carrot and Spinach in *Goma-ae* Sweet Sesame Dressing

This sweet sesame dressing goes with virtually any vegetable, so you are free to choose any combination of vegetables you wish. Vegetables such as bok choy, eggplant, green beans, or burdock root work well. The choice is endless.

Serves four

Carrot:

- 1 carrot
- 3 Tbsp black sesame seeds
- 2 Tbsp maple syrup
- 2 tsp soy sauce

Spinach:

- 1 bunch spinach, about 12 oz. (350 g)
- A pinch salt
- 3 Tbsp white sesame seeds
- 2 Tbsp maple syrup
- 2 tsp soy sauce

1 Peel the carrot. Cut into 2-in. (5-cm) lengths and then into ⅓-in. (8-mm) sticks. Blanch in boiling water 5 to 7 minutes, until tender but crunchy, and drain in a sieve.

2 Pulse the black sesame seeds in a food processor until the seeds are ground, but still a little chunky. Add the maple syrup and soy sauce, and pulse a few times to mix. Combine the black sesame mixture with the carrots.

3 If the spinach has roots attached, trim but don't remove—just vigorously rinse in cold running water. Blanch in boiling water with a pinch of salt, slowly sinking the bunch in from the root to the leaves, for 15 seconds. Remove, plunge in ice water to cool, and drain. Squeeze the water out by hand and cut into 2-in. (5-cm) lengths.

4 Pulse the white sesame seeds in a food processor until the seeds are ground but still chunky. Add the maple syrup and soy sauce, and pulse a few times to mix. Squeeze any water out of the spinach again and combine with the sesame mixture.

5 Arrange the two kinds of dressed vegetables on a serving plate.

Niku Jaga Simmered Potato and Beef

There are a lot of variations on this home standard. You could use beef cubes instead of thin slices, but it is better to try finding a butcher who will slice beef thinly. Dining on thin slices dressed in the sauce, eaten with the meltingly soft simmered onions, is one of the best ways to enjoy good, tender beef.

Serves four

4 medium potatoes, preferably russet
8 green beans
½ onion
3 ½ oz. (100 g) beef, sliced thinly (any tender cut of beef works)
1 tsp olive oil or roasted sesame oil
2 Tbsp maple syrup or sugar
3 Tbsp soy sauce

1 Peel the potatoes and cut into 4 to 6 equal pieces. Cut the green beans into 1 ⅔-in. (4-cm) lengths. Peel the onion and cut into thin slices. Cut the beef into bite-size pieces.

2 Add the olive oil in a medium saucepan over medium heat and cook the beef until the color just changes. Add the onion and potatoes and cook for 5 minutes. Barely cover with water. Add the maple syrup, bring to a simmer, and cook until the potatoes become tender, about 15 minutes.

3 Add the green beans and soy sauce, and simmer for 4 to 5 minutes. Check the taste and adjust with maple syrup, soy sauce, or water to taste.

NOTES

- During the simmering, first add the sweetener (maple syrup or sugar), then soy sauce to achieve the right balance between sweetness and saltiness.

Kimpira Sautéed Vegetables with Hot Chili Peppers

Vegetable stew is one of my favorites, but I also like to eat vegetables that still have their crunchy texture. Many Japanese think *kimpira* can only be made with carrots and burdock root, but I think this *kimpira* made with western vegetables is surprisingly good. I enjoy serving many kinds of *kimpira* on the table at once, so that diners can compare the different textures and flavors of the vegetables.

Serves four

■ Parsnip

- 1 parsnip, preferably organic
- 1 red hot chili pepper, fresh or dried
- 1 Tbsp olive oil
- 1 tsp maple syrup
- 2 tsp soy sauce
- 1 tsp sake

1 Scrub any dirt off the parsnip. (If using non-organic parsnip, peel before cutting.) Cut into ⅓-in. (8-mm) slices at an angle. Stack the slices, press them a little to keep them together, and cut into thin sticks.

2 Put the olive oil in a medium saucepan over medium heat. Tear the chili pepper into halves, toss into the pan, and cook until fragrant. Add the parsnip and stir until a little softened, then add the maple syrup, soy sauce, and sake. Cook, shaking the pan from time to time to prevent scorching, until the parsnip is wilted and tender but still crunchy.

■ Bell Peppers

- 5 to 6 red, orange, yellow, or green bell peppers
- 1 red hot chili pepper, fresh or dried
- 1 Tbsp olive oil
- 1 tsp maple syrup or 1 tsp *mirin*
- 2 tsp sake

Halve the bell peppers lengthwise, remove the seeds, and cut into thin sticks. The bell peppers contain a lot of water, so I haven't included sake in this recipe. Cook the bell peppers the same way as the parsnip.

■ Celery

- 2 stalks celery, with leaves intact
- 1 red hot chili pepper, fresh or dried
- 1 Tbsp olive oil
- 1 tsp maple syrup
- 2 tsp soy sauce

Peel the tough strings off the celery stalk and cut into ⅛-in. (3-mm) slices at an angle. Cut the leaves into pieces. Sake is not required for celery. Cook the same way as the parsnip.

■ Lotus root

- A 3-in. (10-cm) piece lotus root
- 1 red hot chili pepper
- 1 Tbsp olive oil
- 1 tsp maple syrup
- 2 tsp soy sauce
- 1 tsp rice vinegar

Peel the lotus root and cut into ⅛-in. (3-mm) rounds. Cook as per the parsnip, using *mirin*, soy sauce, and rice vinegar.

NOTES

■ Dry roots such as parsnip, carrot, and burdock root require sake during sautéing to make *kimpira*.

If root vegetables such as parsnip, carrot, or lotus root are organically grown, there is no need to peel them.

The natural shape of the sliced parsnip will give the sticks a tapered shape after cutting, allowing the narrow ends to become soft and tender while cooking.

Udon Noodles with *Goma-dare* Sesame Dipping Sauce

There are many noodle dishes in Japan, and they all make excellent, quick meals. *Udon* noodles are a regular ingredient in most peoples' pantries and are fast and easy to prepare. This is my favorite lunch recipe. The thick sesame dipping sauce tastes sweet and the soy sauce adds a pleasantly salty taste, making a perfect accompaniment to the noodles.

Serves four

10 oz. (280 g) semi-dried *udon* noodles, or 14 oz. (400 g) dried *udon* noodles
Radish sprout and chopped scallion
Chopped *shiso* leaves (optional)
Shichimi spice powder (optional)

Sesame Dipping Sauce

- 1 cup *dashi* stock (*see* page 146), or water
- 1/4 cup sake
- 1/4 cup soy sauce
- 2 Tbsp. maple syrup or 1/4 cup *mirin*
- 1/3 cup sesame paste

1 For the sesame dipping sauce: Combine the sake and *mirin* in a medium saucepan and bring to a gentle simmer for 1 minute to evaporate the alcohol. Cool to room temperature and combine with the sesame paste.

2 Bring a large pot of water to a boil. Cook the udon noodles until tender but firm to the bite, referring to the package directions, and arrange in a serving bowl with the cooking water. Arrange the sprout, scallion, and *shiso* leaves in a separate bowl.

Udon noodles are made from wheat flour and salt, so there is no need to add salt to the water when boiling. One thing to keep in mind is to boil the noodles until just tender yet firm. Over-boiling results in a mushy, unpleasant texture.

When eating, add the vegetables to the sesame sauce and sprinkle with *shichimi* spice powder if desired. Dip the noodles into the sauce while they are still hot.

名物
七味

Nitsuke Simmered Fish in Soy Sauce and *Dashi* Stock

Nitsuke simmered fish is a typical Japanese way of enjoying tender, flaky fish. You will need to find impeccably fresh fish, because it is meant to cook in its own juices and any flavor that is off will become concentrated and very noticeable. *Wakame* seaweed can be substituted with many kinds of vegetables. I recommend using spinach or chard, or even blanched potato or daikon radish, which will soak up the tasty cooking liquid and become tender and flavorsome.

Serves four

3 heaping Tbsp dried *wakame* seaweed (optional)
4 cod fillets, 5 oz. (140 g) each, skin-on (or any white fish such as flounder, fluke, or sea bream)
4 slices ginger
1 cup water
¼ cup soy sauce
½ cup sake
¼ cup maple syrup
½ bunch scallions, cut into 2-in. (5-cm) lengths
½ cup ginger shreds

1 Soak the dried *wakame* seaweed, if using, in plenty of water for 15 minutes. It will eventually reach up to 8 times or more its dry volume. Rinse in cold running water and drain well. Cut the frilly parts of the *wakame* off the rib if attached. Chop the *wakame* frills into bite-sized pieces.

2 Chose a large pan that will fit all of the fillets in a single layer. Add the ginger, water, soy sauce, sake, and maple syrup to the pan and bring to a gentle simmer. Add the fish fillets skin-side up, and spoon the mixture over the skin so that the skin will not stick to the drop-lid. Bring to a gentle simmer, covered with a drop-lid (see NOTES), and cook for 7 to 8 minutes.

3 Remove the fish fillets and ginger slices from the pan and add the scallions and *wakame* seaweed. Cook for 1 to 2 minutes until they are heated through.

4 Arrange the *wakame* seaweed in a shallow bowl and top with the fish fillets and scallions. Spoon the cooking liquid over the dish and garnish with the ginger shreds.

NOTES

- If you don't have a wooden drop-lid that fits inside the pan, simply use double-layered aluminum foil shaped to fit the inside of the pan.

Dried *wakame* is reconstituted before use. You can buy bags of dried *wakame* pre-cut into small pieces, as it expands during cooking.

When using whole *wakame*, you need to cut off the tough rib that runs along one edge. They can be used as one of the ingredients in the miso soup.

rice & miso soup

Tuna and Avocado Rice Bowl

Avocado, like olive oil, complements the delicate leanness of raw tuna. Both avocado and olive oil have plenty of good monounsaturated fat and Vitamin E, so the combination as a topping for rice is tasty, high in iron, and surprisingly healthy. You can also omit the rice and serve just the topping as an appetizer with a glass of wine or sake.

Wasabi's heat immediately dissipates when combined with oil, so for people who like hot wasabi, I recommend putting a little extra mound on top just before serving.

Serves four

10 oz. (280 g) fresh or frozen yellowfin tuna, any part
2 ripe avocadoes
1 Tbsp lemon juice
2 Tbsp chopped chive
2 tsp extra-virgin olive oil
2 tsp soy sauce
$1\frac{1}{2}$ tsp wasabi paste
4 servings cooked short-grain rice, warm

1 Thaw the tuna if frozen (see details on page 32). Cut the fresh tuna into 1-in. (2-cm) cubes. Cut the avocado in half lengthwise around the pit, twist open the two halves, and remove the pit by inserting the heel of a heavy knife and twisting it out (a). Cut into 1-in. (2-cm) cubes and sprinkle with the lemon juice (b).

2 Place the tuna in a medium bowl and add the olive oil, soy sauce, wasabi, and chives (c). Lightly fold in the avocado. Spoon the mixture over bowls of cooked rice and serve.

HOW TO PREPARE WASABI

If you are lucky enough to find fresh wasabi root, trim away any black, oxidized parts and shave off the protruding knobs. (Do not peel the grey-green skin.) Carefully remove the green stems on the top end with a paring knife held at a shallow angle, like sharpening a pencil, trying not to waste any of the expensive root part. You can grate all the way to the end of the root, though the last inch (2 cm) or so will be yellowish and not as fragrant. Fresh wasabi stalk wrapped in damp paper towels will keep for a month in a refrigerator. You can also freeze wasabi wrapped in plastic wrap, though the taste and texture will be altered.

Garlic Steak Rice Bowl

The really wonderful part of this dish is not the beef, but how the fried rice absorbs the beef juices and garlic-scented oil. The partial browning of the rice, made easier by adding soy-sauce, makes it even more delicious. For fried rice dishes, it is usually better to use cold leftover rice, but I recommend using hot, just-cooked rice for this recipe to enjoy the contrast of the crunchy browned parts and fluffiness of the white parts. This is a great dish when you are hungry, and goes well with an ice-cold beer in the heat of summer.

Serves four

A 10-oz. (300-g) beef steak, ½ in. (1.5 cm) thick
1 Tbsp plus more olive oil
4 cloves garlic, sliced
4 bowls cooked rice
1 bunch watercress, cut into 2-in. (5-cm) lengths
1 Tbsp soy sauce
⅓ tsp ground black pepper

1 Over low heat in a large frying pan, heat the olive oil and garlic until fragrant and light gold, then remove the garlic from the pan and set aside.

2 Turn the heat to medium-high and add the beef steak. Fry—not touching—until the meat loosens from the pan and is nicely browned. Turn it over and fry until the other side is also nicely browned. Remove the steak from the frying pan, place on a wire rack, and allow to rest. Cut the steak into 1-in. (2.5-cm) wide strips.

3 Add a little more olive oil to the pan at medium-high heat. Add the cooked rice and stir fry for 5 minutes (a). Sprinkle the soy sauce and black pepper over the rice and continue to cook, lightly pressing the rice down with a flat spatula against the pan from time to time, until golden brown (b). Add the beef and fried garlic, stir-fry briefly, then add the watercress and swirl once. Divide the mixture into individual bowls and serve.

NOTES

- Any cut of beef that makes good steak, such as rib-eye, striploin, top sirloin, or tenderloin, will work for this dish.

Chirashi Mixed Sushi Rice

Serves four

½ cup dried *hijiki* seaweed (optional)

Soboro egg:

- 3 eggs, plus 1 egg yolk
- 2 Tbsp maple syrup
- 1 Tbsp sake
- A pinch salt

3 ½ oz. (100 g) snow peas
3 green beans
¼ carrot
1 tsp sake for blanching vegetables
1 tsp salt for blanching vegetables
4 servings sushi rice (Recipe on page 142)
3 Tbsp white sesame seeds

1 If using, soak the dried *hijiki* seaweed in plenty of water for 20 minutes, and drain in a sieve. If the seaweed is too long, cut into bite-size pieces.

2 For the *soboro* egg: beat the eggs and egg yolk in a bowl and add the maple syrup, sake, and salt, and mix well. Heat a frying pan over low heat and pour in the egg mixture. Using chopsticks, scramble the mixture finely, scraping the bottom of the pan (a), (b). Set aside.

3 In a medium saucepan, bring plenty of water to a boil and add the salt and sake. Remove the strings from the snow peas. Cut the green beans at an angle into thin slices. Cut the carrot into thin sticks. Blanch in turn the snow peas, green bean slices, and carrot, and drain on a wire rack.

4 Fold the green beans, carrot, *hijiki* seaweed, and white sesame seeds into the sushi rice (c), serve in a large dish and top with the snow peas.

Hijiki seaweed is a great source of fiber.

NOTES

- I scramble the *soboro* egg with four wooden chopsticks held in one hand, which I think is the best way to make finely scrambled eggs. A metal whisk may scratch the pan's surface, and the egg's color will not be as bright yellow. If the scrambled eggs remain too lumpy, a food processor can be used.

a

b

c

Miso Soup of Steamer Clams

The patterns on clam shells differ from place to place, and their endless variety provides a natural beauty. This simple miso soup relies completely on the clams for flavor and the clamshells for visual appeal, and does not require any additional flavoring or garnish.

Add the miso to a ladle, mix, with some of the broth from this recipe to form a loose paste, and sink the ladle into the rest of the soup, swirling to dissolve the paste little by little to prevent lumps. Be careful not to boil the soup after adding the miso, or the subtle savoriness and complex aroma of miso become sour and harsh.

Serves four

1 lb. plus 1 oz. (500 g) live steamer clams

2 Tbsp yellow miso (adjust the amount depending on the saltiness of the miso)

1 Lightly rinse the clams in cold running water and place in a bowl. Pour salted water (the basic ratio is 2 cups water and 1 Tbsp salt) halfway covering the clams (a), cover with plastic wrap, poke holes in the wrap with bamboo skewers, and refrigerate from 2 hours to overnight to allow the clams to expel their sand.

2 Drain the clams and rinse in cold running water. Place the clams in a medium saucepan and pour in 4 cups water, or enough to cover. Bring to a gentle simmer over medium heat for 10 minutes until the clams release a white, cloudy broth. Discard any clams that don't open and skim with a strainer (b).

3 Mix in the miso paste (c) and stop the heat just before it begins to simmer. (Never allow the soup to simmer after adding the miso.)

a

b

c

NOTES

- I've found that clams expel their sand better when half-covered with water rather than fully submerged. They also need a dark and cool place to expel sand, and the refrigerator is best. If you have a flat tray with a deep rim and a wire rack that fits into the tray, you can lay the clams in a single layer on the rack instead of using a bowl. The expelled sand will drop though the rack onto the tray, leaving the clams clean.

Miso Soup of Pork Slices and Root Vegetables

Root vegetables seem to grant a kind of natural power taken from the fertile soil they grow in. Carrots and potatoes, familiar in the West, along with Japanese daikon radish and burdock root, are a satisfying combination. Simmering them with sliced pork until tender but still a little crunchy, then stirring in rich miso paste makes the most hearty and fortifying soup I can imagine. You can omit the pork from the soup and use a vegetable stock based on *kombu* kelp and dried mushrooms to make the classic vegan soup enjoyed by Zen monks to ward off the winter cold. Feel free to use turnips, onions, parsnips, or any combination of root vegetables, and be sure not to overcook them, so they retain their texture.

Serves six to eight

1 carrot
A 6-in. (15-cm) thick cylinder cut from a daikon radish
1 *gobo* burdock root
2 to 3 medium potatoes (any variety)
1 scallion
5 oz. (150 g) pork slices
2 Tbsp roasted sesame oil
6 ¼ cups (1.5 L) water or *dashi* stock
⅓ cup yellow miso (adjust the amount depending on the saltiness of the miso)

1 Peel the carrot, cut in half lengthwise, and cut into ⅛-in. (3-mm) thick half moons. Peel the daikon, cut into quarters lengthwise, and cut into ⅛-in. (3-mm) thick wedges. Scrub off any dirt from the burdock root and cut at an angle into ovals. Cut the pork slices into bite-size pieces.

2 Put the roasted sesame oil in a large pot over medium heat and cook the pork slices until they lose their raw, pink color. Add the carrot, daikon radish, burdock root, and potatoes and cook until a little softened. Add the water or *dashi* stock, bring to a gentle simmer, and cook for 15 minutes, skimming from time to time, until all the ingredients are tender, but still a little crunchy.

3 Meanwhile, cut the scallion into thin rounds.

4 Add the scallion, mix in the miso paste, and stop the heat just before simmering. (Never allow to simmer after adding the miso.) Ladle into individual soup bowls and sprinkle *shichimi* spice powder over each serving, if desired.

Miso Soup of Snow Peas

The belly of *niboshi* sardines is very bitter and should be discarded. If you don't have time to soak the sardines, put them in a pot along with water and simmer for 20 minutes.

Everyone enjoys this miso soup, with its pleasant, smoky flavor and rich *umami* taste of *niboshi* dried sardines. The better-known *dashi* stock made from *katsuo* bonito flakes and *kombu* kelp is rather expensive, so it is more practical for most Japanese to use cheaper *niboshi* for everyday soup. I use 7 to 8 small *niboshi* per serving.

Serves four

About 30 small *niboshi* dried sardines, 1 ½ oz. (40 g)
5 ½ oz. (150 g) snow peas
2 Tbsp yellow miso (adjust the amount depending on the saltiness of the miso)

1 Pull off the belly part of the *niboshi* dried sardines and soak in 4 cups of water in a refrigerator overnight (or for 8 hours).

2 Remove the strings from the snow peas, soak in ice water to crisp, and drain.

3 Strain the liquid from the dried sardines with a fine-mesh strainer (discarding the sardines), transfer the liquid to a medium saucepan and bring to a gentle simmer. Add the snow peas and cook for 2 minutes. Mix in the miso paste and stop the heat just before the miso begins to simmer. (Never allow the soup to simmer after adding the miso.) Ladle into individual soup bowls.

desserts

Apple and Citrus Compote

Fuji, a cross-breed with red delicious, is the most popular variety of apple in Japan. Fuji apples are generally not suitable for cooking, but quick-simmering allows them to release their aroma without falling apart, making a great compote. I use *yuzu* citrus because of its unique flavor, but lemon, orange, tangerine, or any kind of citrus will work as well. I love making this dish; there's something uplifting about the aroma of apples and citrus filling the kitchen.

Use your favorite variety of apple and citrus for the recipe.

Serves four

2 Fuji apples (or any variety that works for apple pie)
2 *yuzu* citrus, preferably unwaxed
⅔ cup or more granulated sugar

1 Peel and core the apples and cut into bite-size pieces. Cut the *yuzu*, unpeeled, into small bite-size pieces.

2 In a shallow, non-reactive saucepan, put the apples and *yuzu*, sprinkle with the sugar, and leave for 20 minutes. During this time, the apple and *yuzu* should release their juices.

3 Bring the pan to a boil over high heat. Lower the heat to medium-high and cook for 15 minutes, until the apples and *yuzu* become translucent. Do not stir, but shake the pan from time to time. With a ladle, carefully remove any white foam that forms on the surface.

4 Cool to room temperature and serve. Keeps 5 to 6 days in a refrigerator.

Do not stir the mixture, but rather shake the pan periodically.

NOTES

- Use a shallow pan so that the water evaporates quickly and the shape of the ingredients remains intact. In a deep pot the apple will steam and fall apart into an unpleasant, soggy mess.

Vanilla and Black Sesame Ice Cream

You may already know about black sesame ice cream, since it is popular in Asian restaurants, but if you have not yet tasted the sweet, nutty aroma of this wonderful dessert, you definitely should try—it's a new world of flavor! I prefer a smooth texture, so I grind the sesame seeds into as fine a powder as possible in a food processor. But if you prefer a little crunch, you can grind the seeds partially, leaving some coarser pieces remaining.

Makes about 1 pint

1 pt vanilla ice cream, bought from a store
½ cup (about 2 oz./ 60 g) black sesame seeds

1 Let the ice cream stand at room temperature to soften a little.

2 Grind the sesame seeds in a food processor into the desired texture.

3 Using a rubber spatula, combine the ice cream and ground sesame seeds in a large bowl until mixed evenly. Transfer to a container and freeze well.

The black sesame seeds add a wonderfully deep, nutty flavor to the vanilla ice cream.

NOTES

- Look for black sesame seeds at Asian or Middle-eastern food markets. They often come in bags and are cheaper than those sold in small bottles at specialty stores. If the sesame seeds you find are not yet toasted, toast them until fragrant.

Matcha Green Tea and Milk Jelly

Matcha powdered green tea is an essential feature of the traditional tea ceremony, where it is prepared using a bamboo whisk, and mixed with hot water. When combined with sugar and milk, however, this thick, fragrant, and slightly bitter powder yields a mellow and rounded taste. The recipe for this *matcha* and milk jelly dessert is for serving in individual molds, but you can also make the jelly in a large bowl and scoop out servings, especially fun for casual occasions.

This finely ground, powdered green tea dissolves completely in hot liquid.

Yields four 1/4-cup/50-ml jelly molds

2 ½ Tbsp granulated sugar
1 tsp *matcha* powdered green tea
¼ oz. (7 g) sheet gelatin
(1 envelope=1 Tbsp gelatin powder can be substituted)
1 cup whole milk

Sauce:
3 Tbsp granulated sugar
4 tsp *matcha* powdered green tea
4 Tbsp hot water

1 Combine the sugar and tea powder in a small bowl. Soak the gelatin in plenty of water to hydrate for 10 minutes. (If using powdered gelatin, skip this step and combine with sugar and *matcha* powdered green tea.)

2 Pour the milk in a small saucepan over low heat. When the milk feels a little hot to the skin (or reaches 140°F/60°C), wring the water out of the sheet gelatin by hand and add gelatin to the hot milk. Gently stir using a rubber spatula until it melts. Do not bring to a boil.

3 Pour a little of the milk mixture into the bowl of sugar and powdered green tea, and mix to make a paste. Add the rest of the milk little by little, gently mixing with a rubber spatula. Strain through a fine cloth, such as a gauze, into a separate bowl and pour into individual jelly molds. Cool to room temperature, then refrigerate for 2 hours or more until set.

4 Combine all the ingredients for the sauce and mix thoroughly. Chill in the refrigerator.

5 Dip the mold into warm water, almost to the depth of the jelly, and hold for a few seconds. Lift the mold out of the water, and place a serving dish on top of the mold. Hold the dish and the mold firmly together, and invert the mold to slip the jelly onto the dish. If the jelly does not slip from the mold, dip in water again and repeat the inversion process. Spoon the sauce over each jelly.

NOTES

- There are many varieties of gelatin, but many professionals prefer to use sheet gelatin since it does not need a precise amount of liquid to soften. The weight of one package of sheet gelatin or powder gelatin differs from country to country, and from brand to brand. I have seen sheet weights of 2.5 to 3.5 g, so always measure gelatin by weight, not by package.
- For powdered gelatin, the American brand Knox has ¼ oz. (7 g) per envelope, which yields 2½ to 3 tsp. The British brand Dr. Oetker has 11 g gelatin powder in an envelope. Generally speaking, ¼ oz. (7 g) of gelatin can coagulate about 2 cups (500 ml) of liquid, and you do not need to worry so much about subtle differences in weight. To soften powdered gelatin, you sometimes need to use some liquid from the recipe, but here you can just add the powdered gelatin to the milk by mixing with the sugar.

White Lima Beans in Maple Syrup

Allow the beans soak up plenty of water.

Sweetened bean-based desserts are not found in Western cuisine, but every time I serve this dish in Europe or North America, my friends love it. Giant white beans, called *shiro-hana-mame* in Japan and Fagioli Bianchi di Spagna in Italy, have a slight buttery flavor that is deliciously highlighted by whipped cream. This dessert goes wonderfully with leaf-brewed English tea (or with good, hot coffee).

Serves four

3 ½ oz. (100 g) dried giant white lima beans (butter beans)
2 cups extra light maple syrup
2 cups whipped heavy cream
4 tsp maple sugar

1 Soak the beans in plenty of water in a large, deep pot or bowl, and place in a refrigerator overnight (or at least 8 hours).

2 Drain the beans in a sieve and return to the pot. Cover with fresh water (the water should reach 4 in./10 cm above the level of the beans) and bring to a boil over high heat. Lower the heat, and gently simmer for 1 ½ to 2 hours until the beans are tender. Cool the beans in the simmering liquid until tepid. Measure 2 cups of the beans for use. Divide the rest of the beans—with the liquid—into small freezer bags or containers and store in the freezer.

3 Drain the 2 cups of beans. Combine with the maple syrup in a bowl and refrigerate for 1 hour to allow the beans to absorb the syrup.

4 Serve the beans and maple syrup in a serving bowl with a large spoon. Serve the whipped cream and maple sugar in separate bowls with spoons. To eat, scoop up the beans and syrup with a spoon and top with the whipped cream and maple sugar to taste.

Guests can help themselves to as much or as little as they like. The dessert is eaten with a small spoon.

Whiskey-marinated Kiwi and *Yokan* Bean Jelly

Yokan is a popular dessert—sweetened red bean paste set in a mold with agar-agar, a seaweed-based gelatin. We serve slices of it as part of the tea ceremony, and also give it as a neatly wrapped gift to show gratitude to our friends. I like *yokan* as is, but I find the addition of kiwi fruit marinated in Scotch whiskey perfectly offsets the rich sweetness of the red beans. If you can't find *yokan* in your area, try adding the whiskey-marinated kiwi to a dense chocolate cake.

Whisky-marinated kiwi has a rich and sumptuous taste that is a perfect partner to the *yokan* bean jelly.

Makes eight pieces

- 2 ripe kiwi
- 1 cup Scotch or Scotch-style whiskey, single-malt or blended
- ½ cup granulated sugar
- 1 cup water
- 8 slices *yokan* bean jelly

1 Combine the granulate sugar and water in a small saucepan over low heat to dissolve the sugar completely and make a light syrup. Transfer to a small bowl to cool to room temperature.

2 Cut off the ends of the kiwi, peel off the skin, and cut each into 4 slices. Add the kiwi slices and whisky to the bowl of syrup and refrigerate overnight (at least 8 hours).

3 Arrange the marinated kiwi slices on a serving plate and top each with a slice of *yokan* bean jelly.

NOTES

- Instead of sugar syrup, 1 ½ cup of maple syrup can be used instead.

my home kitchen

the equipment

The average Japanese kitchen of today is much more westernized than when I was growing up. Some, for example, have European-style built-in ovens for the increasing number of home cooks who like to roast large blocks of meat or bake bread and cakes. Yet when it comes to fish, Japanese almost never turn to an oven. Inevitably, they will use the small "fish grill" (actually a broiler) that comes equipped under every range top in every kitchen. At most, this compartment can cook only four slices of salmon at one time, but it's still the instrument of choice.

Even when I'm in Japan, however, I like to cook fish in an oven. There are several reasons for this. One is that I am usually preparing a great many servings at once or roasting a whole fish with Western seasonings. But I'm also well aware of the convenience of ovens: turn on the broil switch to crisp the skin after cooking, and any fish quickly becomes tastier. (And if you have a grill, I suggest you take full advantage of it to cook fish as well as meat. It's a favorite activity of mine when I'm at my home in Umbria.)

Dishwashers have yet to become widespread in Japan. This is partly due to space limitations but also because much of Japanese tableware—earthenware dishes, lacquerware bowls, and wooden chopsticks, for instance—is not dishwasher safe. Switching to porcelain and Western-style dishes would solve the problem, but given the significance in Japanese cuisine to appreciating the feel of vessels in the hands or against the lips, many would find something seriously

lacking in a table set entirely with porcelain. A dishwasher should under no circumstances be used on kitchen cutlery, either, since heat will alter the material and blunt the edge. Instead, develop a habit of rinsing each knife in water immediately after use.

Among smaller kitchen utensils, I use a Cuisinart food processor to grind sesame seeds instead of the traditional *suribachi* mortar. Likewise, the task of mashing soybeans for tofu always goes to the Oster blender that I bought many years ago. But there are a few traditional Japanese utensils that will never be replaced. The gentle touch of wooden cooking chopsticks is a must when scrambling eggs in a pan, turning over fish, or cooking tempura. A wooden *otoshibuta* drop lid rests on top of simmering liquids, distributing heat evenly and applying just enough weight to prevent foods from jostling and breaking up. Cutting boards should be of wood, too, in order to absorb the shock on the knife blade.

Kitchen knives

The Global brand of kitchen knives also sells specialized water whetstones that make its products easy to sharpen and maintain, even for amateur cooks. Merging the blade and handle means enhanced hygiene. I mainly use, from left to right, the Slicer (blade length 8.4 in./21 cm) to slice fish, the Cooking Knife (8 in./20 cm), and the Petty Knife (4 in./10 cm).

Mandolin slicer

While I use knives for the bulk of my fine slicing work, this tool is indispensable when I need to efficiently shred a large amount of vegetables. It's especially convenient for recipes such as *Gari* Ginger Pickles (page 38).

Spider strainer

This useful tool enables you to remove deep-fried foods from oil several pieces at a time, as opposed to individually with tongs or chopsticks. A finer-meshed spider can be used to pick up small bits of food or to skim off scum.

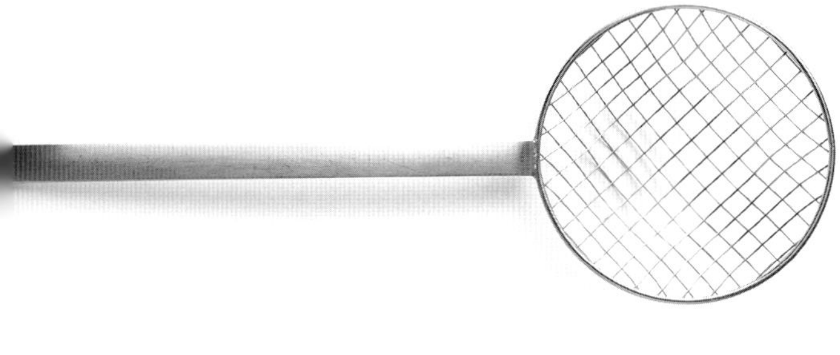

Wooden cutting boards

A wooden board is essential to protecting knives, since even the toughest blade will be ruined on a plastic cutting board. I had these boards custom-developed after discovering that my favorite U.S.-made parquet board was unavailable in Japan. The rubberwood panels are 10½ in. (26 cm) square each and can be flexibly combined: I use one for small tasks such as chopping garlic, and lay out four to cut long vegetables or to fillet fish. The boards are thick and stable and fit snugly together. I also make sure to wash and dry well immediately after use. (For inquiries contact La Base, page 152.)

Stick grater

Graters by Microplane are outstanding: zesting lemon with this tool produces a lacy, fluffy mass of rind that instantly gives an attractive finishing touch to *nimono* (simmered foods) or any other dish. It can also grate *shoga* ginger and garlic, both frequently required in Japanese cooking. The company offers a range of graters with various blades, but the Zester/Grater fits virtually any purpose.

Japanese grater

But not even the Zester/Grater can grate daikon radish the way it should be done. For this task, you need a traditional Japanese grater with teeth that sink deeply into the daikon—just be careful it doesn't also slice through your fingers! The tool performs just as well on *shoga* and garlic, too, of course. I use a copper grater by Aritsugu that is roughly 10 in./25 cm long, including the handle.

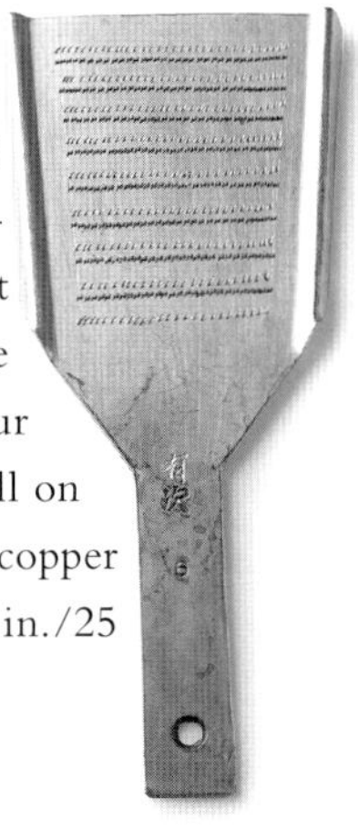

Serving spoon

When you're transferring food from a pot or pan to a dish, a serving spoon that's shallower than a ladle helps you do an attractive job. I designed this spoon based on an aluminum spoon that I came across in Vietnam. With a bowl about 4 in. (10 cm) long and 2½ in. (6 cm) wide, my spoon is made of stainless steel but with a black coating that makes it a pleasing table accent as well. (La Base.)

Food processor

The usefulness of this tool goes without saying. As mentioned before, it's excellent for grinding sesame seeds, and hardly a day goes by without my using it to prepare one Japanese-style dish or another. I let my Cuisinart take care of mincing onions and garlic as well.

Wooden chopsticks

The above chopsticks are for handling grilled or broiled foods. They're more than 12 in. (30 cm) long, well balanced, and rest solidly in the hand. The tips are square for gripping food, perfect for lifting fish or vegetables to turn over as they cook. The wood is hard and surprisingly resistant to burning. Below are serving chopsticks with pointed tips to facilitate precise work. They're suited to picking up tiny beans or a pinch of delicate herb. The bevel at the end is for scooping up dabs of miso, wasabi, grated ginger, and other pastes.

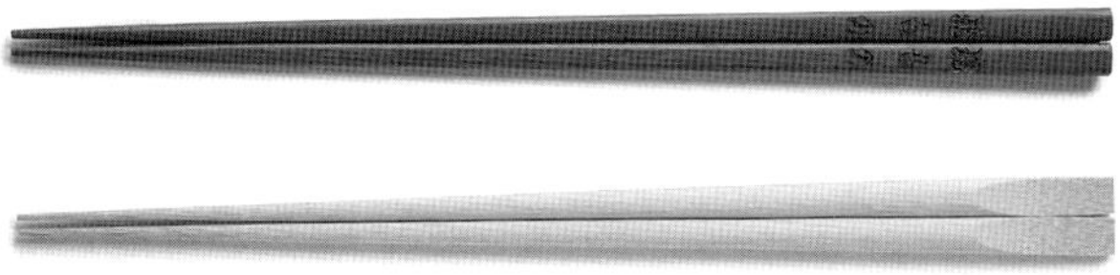

Stick blender

I love this type of blender for its convenience. When making mayonnaise or dressing, I just insert the stick blender into a tall container and mix, then wash the end with running water immediately after. It is also great for mixing simmered vegetables in a pot for a cream soup.

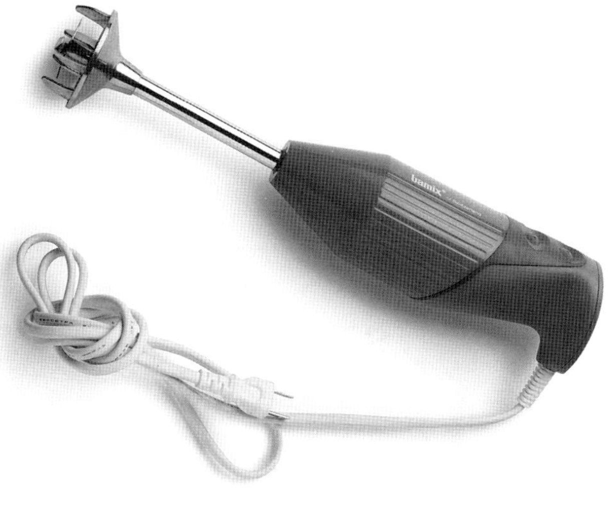

***Sarashi* cotton cloth and gauze (page 128)**

Sarashi cotton cloth (below) is indispensable for fine sifting, such as when filtering *dashi* stock, or straining the soybean mixture when making tofu. In Japan, it is often sold in rolls of 33 ft. (10 m) × 14 in. (34 cm). The desired length is then cut. Gauze (above) is also made from cotton, but woven more roughly than *sarashi* cloth. Gauze is good for wrapping fish fillets when marinating with miso, for making a herb sachet, or for lining when steaming food to prevent it sticking to the bottom of the pan.

Rectangular Tray, Mesh tray, Rectangular lid/plate

Shallow, rectangular cooking trays such as those shown here are commonly found in Japanese kitchens. A sizable flat-bottomed tray is especially desirable when you want to marinate fish or vegetables without losing their shape. When deep-frying, lining up three trays each filled with flour, eggs, and breadcrumbs smoothes the process. Fit one of these with a mesh tray of matching size, and you can drain oil from the deep-fried food. The photographs show, from left to right, a $8\frac{1}{2} \times 10$-in. (21×25-cm) tray with a depth of about $1\frac{2}{3}$ in. (4 cm), a mesh tray of matching size, and a $\frac{1}{2}$-in. (1-cm) deep rectangular plate. To drain tofu, for example, set the mesh tray into the regular tray, place a block of tofu wrapped in cloth, and weight it down with a lid. (La Base. page 152.)

Bowl, Meshed Bowl, Round lid/plate

The bowl pictured below has a rim specially designed to ensure dripless pouring. It is particularly convenient to have a finely meshed bowl that can be fitted closely over another regular bowl to dry foods after rinsing. You can shift the flour, or strain the stock with the mesh bowl. The fitted lid is very versatile and can also be used as a plate. (La Base.)

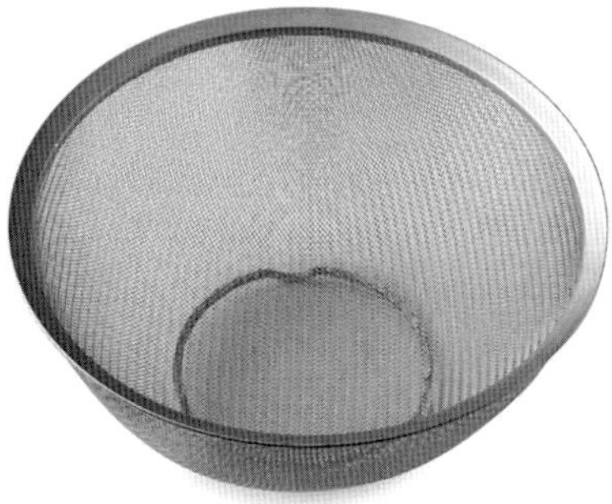

Otoshibuta Drop Lid

While it's possible to simmer foods without a wooden *otoshibuta* drop lid, having one makes a huge difference. The lid provides just the right weight and absorbency to perfectly distribute flavor throughout the ingredients—even when using very little liquid. Use one to simmer foods that break apart easily, such as fish or potatoes. Be sure to soak the lid for a short time in water before using.

Tongs

Although not a traditional Japanese cooking utensil, the tongs have gained popularity in recent years, and are now a must-have in the kitchen. Their variety of uses includes picking up and flipping large pieces of meat with precision on a grill or in an oven, lifting pasta noodles, or mixing salads. Types that can be locked closed after use are convenient and can be stored easily.

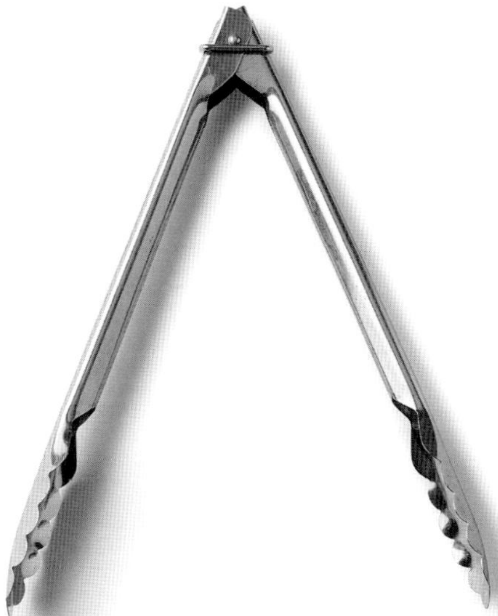

seasonings

Oil

Oils are crucial to cooking, since food cannot be heated effectively without them. Because they are also used as a seasoning, it is even more important to select high quality ones with significant health and beauty benefits. For Japanese food I often use olive oil, which contains large amounts of oleic acid (a monounsaturated fatty acid), and roasted sesame oil, which is rich in vitamins and minerals. I particularly prefer olive oil for deep-frying because of its oxidization-resistant properties. Use extra-virgin olive oil as much as possible in dishes that aren't heated.

Soy sauce

Soy sauce is made by pickling steamed soybeans and parched wheat grains in brine and allowing them to ferment. Naturally brewed, it is rich in lactic-acid bacteria and *umami*, that elusive, uniquely Japanese flavor. Regular soy sauce has a salt content of about 16 to 17 percent and can be salty if used excessively, but in appropriate amounts it imparts a fragrance and savor that cannot be gained from cheaper substitutes that contain additives like caramel coloring and amino acids. The term "soy sauce" in this book indicates the regular type of soy sauce.

Miso

The spread of macrobiotics has made it easier for people to obtain high-quality miso—and there's a special deliciousness to miso created with painstaking care by small-scale brewers. Like soy sauce, miso is fermented and therefore alive; the better the miso, the more important it is to keep it refrigerated instead of at room temperature. Miso is produced in a range of colors using several different ingredients, and choosing between them is a matter of personal preference. I use a blend of two types—standard, all-purpose Shinshu miso (yellow miso) and another, somewhat light-colored, sweet variety. I store them in one container partitioned by a length of *kombu* kelp.

Maple syrup

I often cook with maple syrup. In particular, it's an ideal ingredient for teriyaki sauce because the high boiling point keeps the sauce from burning. The syrup also works surprisingly well as a replacement for *mirin*, given that the true kind (called *hon-mirin*) is still much harder to obtain outside Japan than imitation *mirin*-type seasonings with added sweeteners.

永寶屋
和右衛門
会津吟選しょうゆ
林合名会社
玉締
ごま油
一番しぼり
NET 800g

Hon-mirin

Hon-mirin (true *mirin*) is a sake brewed from steamed glutinous rice. It contains about 13 percent alcohol as well as plenty of natural sweetness and *umami* flavors, and imparts foods not only these two qualities of sweetness and flavor, but also luster. Seasoning with *hon-mirin* gives teriyaki and *nimono* (simmered foods) a gentle sheen that inspires a renewed appreciation of the delicate beauty of Japanese food. In most cases, *mirin* is boiled briefly to evaporate excess alcohol. If you can't get the genuine kind, try maple syrup instead, or perhaps a mixture of three parts sake and one part sugar.

Sake

Sake is brewed from steamed rice. Adding a little of this colorless liquid to food does much to improve flavor, in the same way that a touch of grape wine or Shaoxing rice wine does in other cuisines. An alcohol content of about 15 percent makes sake suited to reducing the raw smell of ingredients while preserving their natural taste. It plays an important role in the preparatory stages of recipes such as the Sautéed Squid in Butter and Soy Sauce (page 46).

Rice vinegar

Vinegar is proof that, above all, thorough, assiduous care during production is what leads to quality taste. This is true of rice vinegar as well as other types such as wine vinegar, maple vinegar, or balsamic vinegar. Artificial vinegar is sour but not much else, whereas carefully brewed natural vinegar is not only sour, but also sweet, flavorful, and full of complex aroma.

Salt

I usually cook with sea salt, and because Japan is surrounded by ocean, I have a whole variety from which to choose. Aside from domestic brands, *fleur de sel* salt from Guérande in France also goes well with Japanese food.

cooking tips and supplemental recipes

RICE

Rice and miso soup are essential at the Japanese dining table, and preparing the rice is the very first task when cooking a meal. Whether we use a pot or an electric rice cooker, we first wash the rice, then let it soak to absorb water. While the rice is soaking, we prepare one of the dishes that will, with the rice, make up the meal. Then, while the rice is cooking, we make another of the meal's dishes. And, finally, while letting the rice stand and steam for a while after cooking, we can focus on the last dish. As you can see, the entire preparation of the meal is built around the basic rhythm of cooking rice.

White Rice

Serves four

2 cups short grain rice
2 cups plus 3 Tbsp water (about 10 % more water than rice)

1 Put the rice in a large bowl with enough cold water to cover the rice and gently stir in a circular motion by hand. The water will turn cloudy. Quickly dump the rice out into a sieve. Repeat this process two or three times.

2 Return the washed rice to the bowl, add enough new water to cover the rice, and let soak for 20 minutes.

3 Drain the rice and place the rice and the measured amount of water in a medium-size, heavy saucepan (preferably enameled cast iron). Cover the pan and cook over medium-high heat. When steam begins to escape, or you hear the lid rattling, reduce the heat to low and cook for another 15 to 20 minutes. Increase the heat to high for a few seconds, then remove from heat and let stand for 5 minutes with the lid on.

4 Uncover the pot and gently cut and fold the rice with a flat rice paddle or spatula, bringing the rice up from the bottom to the top to release steam. Do not stir or mix forcefully.

5 Serve in separate rice bowls.

Water Amount

Because only two ingredients—rice grains and water—are used, it is natural that the results might differ depending on the variety of rice, its degree of dryness, and even the mineral content of the water. For cooking great rice, adjust the water amount, using the short grain rice and water available, until you're satisfied. A good rule of thumb at the beginning is to add water until it

covers the rice by ½ in. (scant 1 cm). In autumn, when cooking new-crop rice, the water should be a little less (about 10 percent) than normal. On the other hand, rice that is dried out, or left in storage for a long time, needs a little more water. (When making sushi rice, the water should be reduced by about 3 Tbsp, as the sushi vinegar will also hydrate the rice.)

The purpose of washing rice

Rice grains must be washed because of the powdery debris of rice germ and bran that remains after the grains are polished. Modern industrial polishing has improved to the point where washing rice is quick and easy. Stirring the grains under water also acts as a final polishing, making the rice shiny and smooth when cooked. The most important thing to keep in mind when washing rice is to immediately drain the water from the first wash. This water picks up the majority of dirt and debris, and so leaving the rice in it, even for a few extra seconds, will cause a musty, unpleasant smell and taste.

The pot for cooking rice

Choose a heavy pot with a heavy lid. The pot itself needs a thick bottom with good thermal conductivity. I always use a ceramic pot, called a *donabe* in Japanese. But a cast iron pot with an enamel coating, such as those made by Le Creuset and Staub, is excellent, as is a heavy, stainless-steel-clad aluminum pot. The heaviness of the pot is important for holding in the residual heat that should continue to steam the rice after it is removed from the stove.

Adjusting the heat

Well-cooked rice is tender and fully hydrated, firm and not at all mushy, airy and barely sticking together, each grain plump and shining like silver. It is different from good long-grain rice, which is fluffy and separated. There are some key points to cooking good rice.

The pot must first come to a vigorous boil in order to fully mix the rice and water and ensure even cooking. (Four servings of rice should take 10 to 15 minutes to start boiling.) When the steam forcefully jets out between the lid and the pot, then the heat should be reduced to very low. At this point, the rice grains are still not fully cooked and are a bit hard at the center. Over the time spent on low heat, the moisture will reach the heart of the grains slowly and gently. The jetting steam decreases gradually, until finally one weak puff of steam escapes.

Then, the heat is turned to high for the space of two breaths to raise the temperature of the pot for final steaming, and the stove is immediately turned off. Steaming the rice at the end of cooking with only the residual heat of the pot makes the rice plump, glossy, and airy.

I recommend transferring the finished rice to an *ohitsu*, a traditional wooden rice container that maintains just the right moisture and warmth for holding cooked rice. Still, most Japanese today no longer own an *ohitsu*, so we turn the rice over in its cooking pot to keep it warm but aerated. We never stir or mix the rice, which would turn short-grain rice into a miserable gluey lump. Instead, we invert the rice as gently as possible, bringing the bottom up to the top, using a flat wooden rice paddle in a cutting and folding motion.

Sushi Rice

Traditionally, a flat-bottomed, large round wooden tub called a *hangiri* is used for mixing sushi rice. I always use a large plastic bowl, however, since I've found the rice will not stick so much to its surface. Avoid metal bowls, to which rice will stick relentlessly.

Serves four

2 cups short grain rice
2 cups water

Vinegar mix
- ⅓ cup vinegar
- 1⅔ Tbsp sugar
- ⅔ tsp salt

1 Cook the rice following the method on page 140.

2 Combine all ingredients of the vinegar mix in a small saucepan, and bring to a boil. Immediately remove from the heat, and let cool to room temperature.

3 Transfer the hot rice into a large bowl. Pour over the vinegar mix and distribute evenly by moving the spatula flat in a cutting motion, sometimes folding the rice. Do not mix or stir or the rice will become sticky.

Brown Rice

I grew up eating brown rice, and still have a taste for it. It goes so well with dishes based on olive oil or butter that I almost always use it when I'm abroad. Cooking it requires special pots, however. The Ohsawa pot is a pressure cooker insert made of earthenware, designed especially for brown rice. The far-infrared rays generated by the heated pot make the brown rice plump and juicy, and not at all dry. It is popular among macrobiotic diet practitioners in Japan. On the other hand, the texture of brown rice cooked directly in a pressure cooker is a little more sticky and chewy—a texture many Japanese enjoy.

Brown Rice with Ohsawa Pot and Pressure Cooker

Serves six

3 cups brown rice
3 cups water

1 Wash the rice and drain in a sieve. Put the rice in an Ohsawa pot with the water and cover with the lid. Insert the Ohsawa pot into a pressure cooker and pour in water halfway up the side of the Ohsawa pot. Cover the pressure cooker with a lid.

2 Put the pressure cooker over high heat until it reaches full pressure, leave for 2 to 3 minutes, then reduce the heat to low and cook 50 to 60 minutes.

3 Remove the pressure cooker from the heat and release the pressure by running cold water over it. Remove the Ohsawa pot, open the lid, and fold the rice from the bottom to release the steam.

Brown Rice with Pressure Cooker

Serves six

3 cups brown rice
4 cups water

1 Wash the rice and drain in a sieve. Put the rice and the water in a pressure cooker. Put over high heat until it reaches full pressure, and leave for 2 to 3 minutes. Reduce the heat to low and cook for 20 to 25 minutes.

2 Remove from the heat and release the steam. Fold the rice from the bottom to release the heat.

Dashi Stock

Japanese *dashi* stock is typically taken from one or more of four ingredients that are selected according to purpose: *kombu* kelp, *katsuo bushi* (dried bonito flakes), *niboshi* (small dried sardines), and shiitake mushrooms. Professional chefs usually prepare a *kombu*-and-bonito *dashi* that are used in a wide array of dishes; in most homes, by contrast, *dashi* appears in a more limited number of items, such as miso soup and *nimono* (simmered foods). Given the westernization of Japanese eating habits, very few home cooks make *dashi* every day.

I don't cook Japanese food for every meal either, and I've found that it is most efficient to make a certain amount of *dashi* and freeze what I don't use. This does take away the fragrance, but the flavor remains, so that the *dashi* still works in making *nimono* (pages 97), noodle dip (page 100), or sauce (page 22, 62, and 86). I am convinced, however, that nothing is better than freshly made *dashi* for miso soup and other dishes in which aroma is paramount.

In this book I've tried, as much as possible, to introduce recipes that don't call for *dashi* (or have a variation that can be made without it). But for those interested, I've included an explanation below of how to prepare basic *kombu*-and-bonito *dashi*, and—for vegetarians—another *dashi* using only *kombu*. Once you begin appreciating good *dashi*, you might even want to try making your own bonito flakes by shaving the hardened, dried bonito yourself (though this may be hard to find, depending on where you live).

Since my goal in this book is to show that Japanese home cooking can be simple, good, and healthy, don't be put off just because preparing *dashi* sounds too bothersome. I feel that using the convenient powdered type is a perfectly valid choice, especially since good *dashi* ingredients are still not widely available in the West. There are additive-free types available in Japan, and if you have friends there, you could ask a friend to send some. In the end, the choice is the same as choosing between simmering stock yourself from chicken and herbs versus picking a few packets off the shelf at the supermarket.

Basic *Kombu*-and-bonito *Dashi*

Yields about 2 1/2 quarts (2.4 L)

8-in. (20-cm) strip of dried *kombu* kelp
3 1/2 oz. (100 g) dried bonito flakes
2 3/4 quarts (about 2.6 L) water

1 Place the *kombu* kelp in a large pot of water and let stand about 30 minutes (or overnight in a refrigerator).

2 Place the pot over low heat. Just before the water boils, remove the *kombu* and immediately add the bonito flakes.

3 Turn off heat and press the bonito flakes down into the liquid with cooking chopsticks and leave 5 to 10 minutes while flakes sink to the bottom. The *dashi* stock is ready once the liquid ladled from the center of the pot has acquired the desired flavor.

4 Prepare to strain the *dashi* stock. Dampen a *sarashi* cloth (or gauze or doubled cheesecloth) with water, wring it out as thoroughly as possible, and lay over the strainer. Choose a large pot to receive the *dashi* stock, preferably one just wide enough to fit the cloth-lined strainer over the pot.

5 Pour the *dashi* stock over the strainer, flakes and all. Do not press or squeeze, but wait for the liquid to drain naturally. If not using immediately, let the *dashi* stock cool slightly, separate into portions, and refrigerate or freeze. *Dashi* will last a day if refrigerated, a month if frozen.

NOTES

▪ After draining the *dashi* stock, lightly squeeze out the used bonito flakes, sprinkle with soy sauce, and spread on a baking tray. Toast in an oven at low temperature (300°F/150°C) for about 1 1/2 hours until mostly dry, then gather into a plastic bag and knead out the clumps. Add hot water to make soup for noodles, or sprinkle dry over rice as a delicious topping.

The thickness of the shaved bonito flakes can be adjusted by tapping the blade of the plane with a hammer. I bought the plane shown here at Tokyo's Tsukiji fish market. Like kitchen knives, planes should be purchased from a store that offers comprehensive after-sale service, including blade sharpening and repair. The dried bonito fillets should be stored in a refrigerator or wine cellar, wrapped in plastic. If by any chance the surface turns moldy, simply shave away the affected part.

Kombu Dashi

Yields slightly less than 2 1/2 quarts (2.4 L)

8-in. (20-cm) strip of dried *kombu* kelp
2 1/2 qt. (2.4 L) water

Soak the *kombu* kelp in the water and let stand overnight in a refrigerator. Remove the *kombu* kelp. If not using immediately, separate the *dashi* stock into portions and refrigerate or freeze. The *dashi* will keep until the next day if refrigerated, for a month if frozen.

Deep-frying

As I mentioned on page 54, Japanese-style deep-fried foods are not unhealthy. The method uses high temperatures to take foods to their optimum flavor level, rather than adding fats that will be absorbed by the body. Fried food should always be thoroughly drained on a wire rack, and the food is often served on traditional Japanese *washi* paper as well to absorb any excess oil. This also keeps pieces from turning soggy over time.

Utensils

Pans should be of a thick material that conducts heat well, such as stainless steel, iron, or copper. There are Japanese tempura pans specifically designed to withstand the high temperatures reached by the oil. Woks will do, but the ideal is a flat-bottomed pan that heats oil evenly. Slowly stirring the oil from time to time with cooking chopsticks will help distribute the heat.

Although recipes usually do not indicate it, I will once again stress that a rack for draining oil after frying is essential. I use a rectangular mesh tray fitted over a matching tray (page 134), but a wire rack with a plate underneath will also serve well, and—if none of these is available—you can lay the fried pieces on absorbent paper towels. A rack is preferable, since an equally important purpose of the step is to dissipate heat. Remember that foods continue to cook even after being removed from the oil. Be caeful not to fry pieces too long, particularly seafood.

Oil

Olive oil is my favorite because it fries food crisply and does not oxidize easily. Salad (vegetable) oil, canola oil, soybean oil, or peanut oil are suitable, too; each gives a different flavor, and so can be chosen according to taste. A small amount of sesame oil can also be added if a strong aroma is to your liking.

The fresher the oil, the better the taste of the food. But it's acceptable to reuse oil that has fried ingredients, such as vegetables, that do not taint it strongly. When recycling the oil, let it cool before pouring it into a container and storing it in a cool, dark place with little exposure to air. The oil will still turn rancid eventually, so be sure to use it again within three or four days. Oil used on meat or fish acquires a smell that will transfer to other foods, and should be discarded.

To discard the oil, wait for it to cool before putting wadded newspaper or other waste paper into the pan. After the oil is fully absorbed, place the paper in the trash. Japanese stores sell chemical agents that coagulate used oil for convenient disposal.

Amount of oil

The ideal amount of oil to use is "plenty." By that I mean that the oil should be deep enough for pieces to sink into the oil and then rise to the surface again. While you *can* fry foods in a frying pan in oil as shallow as an inch, the results will be uneven, with some pieces burnt and others raw. Even more of a reason not to do this is the danger that oil might splatter from a too-shallow pan and catch fire. I use a roughly 4-in. (10-cm) deep pan filled to a little over half with oil. If your pan is small, cook in small batches to prevent overcrowding.

Oil temperature

The three basic oil temperatures to keep in mind are low (about 300 to 325°F/150 to 160°C), medium (about 340 to 350°F/170 to 180°C), and high (about 375°F/190°C). Roughly speaking, the temperature is low if you drop a bit of batter or an ingredient in the oil and it sinks, medium if it partly sinks before rising, and high if it sets immediately on the surface without sinking. Of course, beginners may find it easier to actually measure the temperature with a frying thermometer.

A phrase used in Japan to praise deep-fried food is that "the oil drains well"—in other words, that the piece is crisp, not soggy. The best way to achieve this quality is to fry twice, much as you do when taking the time to make good french fries. To begin, fry at low to medium temperature just long enough for the heat to barely penetrate all the way. Without waiting for the piece to brown sufficiently, remove onto a rack and let drain. Next, heat the oil to high temperature and cook again, this time until the surface turns crisp and golden brown. The technique is useful when you're preparing a lot of food, since you can cook everything once in advance, and then refry once your guests have arrived to serve pieces at their piping-hot best.

glossary

For a glossary of very basic seasonings used in Japanese home cooking, please see page 136.

Bitter squash (*goya*)
A warty-looking green squash grown in South and Southeast Asia, China, Africa, and the Caribbean. Hollow on the inside with a fluffy white pith and white seeds. The extremely bitter pith and seeds are scooped out after cutting lengthwise, and the rind is sliced and cooked. It tastes like zucchini with an underlying bitterness, and is very nutritious and refreshing in summer.

Daikon radish
A long, large white radish with a fresh, crispy texture. Eaten raw, grated, or simmered.

***Dashi* stock**
Japanese stock, most often made from dried bonito flakes and *kombu* kelp. See detailed explanation and recipes on page 144.

***Gari* ginger pickles**
Ginger pickled in sweet vinegar, often served as a palate cleanser. Well known as a condiment at sushi restaurants. See homemade *gari* recipe on page 38.

***Hijiki* seaweed**
Sargassum fusiforme, a popular seaweed in Japan and praised among macrobiotic and vegetarian dieters for its nutrition. It is grown on the rocky coastlines of Japan, Korea, and China and has a greenish brown color in the wild; its length ranges from about 20 to 40 in. (50 to 100 cm). It is harvested, steamed, then dried and packed to be sold. It is often sold separated into stalks and leaves, called *naga-hijiki* (for the stalk) and *me-hijiki* (for the leaves), but both can be used in the same way.

Japanese mustard
Made from oriental mustard seeds known for their hotness, unlike the milder yellow mustard seeds used in Western mustard. It comes in powder or paste form. It is not made with vinegar.

***Kabocha* pumpkin**

A winter squash with edible green skin and orange-yellow flesh. When cooked, its flesh becomes tender, smooth, and sweet with a somewhat buttery aroma. An average *kabocha* weighs from 2 to 3 lbs. (900 g to 1.3 kg) and is often sold in wedges. If using whole, cut into halves, remove seeds, then cut into wedges. See details on page 62.

Katakuriko

A popular Japanese pure starch powder used the same way as cornstarch. When used as a coating for frying, it finishes crispier and lighter than cornstarch. Originally made from *katakuri* root (*Erythronium japonicum*, a species of lily) but presently made from potato starch due to a shortage of *katakuri*.

***Kombu* kelp**

Dried seaweed used mainly in *dashi* stock for its abundance of meaty tasting glutamic acid.

Lotus root

Fresh and crispy like celery when raw or pickled, but potato-like when cooked. Found in Asian food markets.

***Matcha* powdered green tea**

Used in the Japanese tea ceremony. Its deep flavor and pleasant bitterness has made it popular among European pastry chefs.

Mimolette cheese

A cow's-milk, semi-hard cheese, made in France, normally weighing about 4½ lbs. (2 kg) in a round shape and sold cut into wedges. The whitish rind should be removed. The orange flesh has a pleasantly salty and aged taste.

***Mizuna* greens**

Feathery salad greens with crispy white stems, found in some specialty food markets or farmer's markets. Baby *mizuna* leaves are often found in mesclun, packs of mixed salad leaves. It tends to quickly wilt, so keep wrapped in damp towels in a plastic bag in the refrigerator. Crisp in ice water before using.

Napa cabbage

Chinese cabbage, sweeter in winter.

***Niboshi* dried sardines**

Small sardines with silvery blue skin, simmered in salted water and dried. A common ingredient for making *dashi* stock. Full of good unsaturated fatty acids, so keep refrigerated or frozen after opening the package. Keeps about six months.

***Nigari* coagulant**

Nigari comes in liquid or powder form, but in Japan, liquid is preferred. It is a byproduct of sea salt manufacturing. When making sea salt, the sodium chloride crystallizes first, and the remaining liquid becomes *nigari*, which contains magnesium chloride, calcium chloride, and other minerals. The content of magnesium chloride depends on the product; some are only 7 percent, while others are 35 percent. You should check the package for the right amount and usage to make the right firmness of tofu.

***Nori* seaweed**

A dried, black seaweed sheet made from pressed, dried, and toasted algae. Regular *nori* sheets are about 7 × 8 in. (18.5 × 20.5 cm), usually sold 10 sheets to a pack.

***Ponzu* sauce**

Tangy, slightly salty, but flavorful sauce made from citrus juice and soy sauce. It is sold in bottles in Asian food markets, but can be made at home. See recipe on page 22.

Sansho

A Japanese pepper, the seeds of the prickly ash tree *Zanthoxymum peperitum*. Both its seeds and leaf buds (*kinome*) are used in a variety of cuisines.

Shabu-shabu

A hot pot in which paper-thin beef slices and vegetables are cooked and served with a dipping sauce. The well-marbled beef slices are briefly swished ("*shabu*" in Japanese) in hot broth for a few seconds and eaten.

Shichimi spice powder
A spice mixture commonly made by mixing chili pepper, sesame seed, poppy seed, hemp seed, *shansho* pepper, dried orange peel, and *nori*.

Shiso leaves
A fragrant, refreshing herb, *Perilla frutescens,* related to basil and mint.

Tarako cod roe
Salted pollock roe, sold in its sac. It is found fresh or frozen in Asian markets. It can be simply grilled as is and eaten by cutting into pieces.

Taro root
A starchy, potato-like tropical tuber with brown, fibrous skin and gray-white (sometimes purple-tinged) flesh. A small round variety, called *satoimo*, is popular in Japan.

Udon noodles
Thick white noodles made of hard wheat flour, salt, and water.

Umami
The savory flavor found in certain amino acids in protein-rich foods. Aged beef, cheese, mushrooms, ripe tomatoes, dried *kombu* kelp, and dried fish all contain rich *umami*.

Wakame seaweed
A seaweed, *Undaria pinnatifida,* that has a deep green color. When cooked, it becomes a brighter green and a little slippery in texture. It is sold fresh or salted in Japan and Korea, but mostly sold dried in Asian markets in western countries. To use dried *wakame*, rehydrate in plenty of water as it swells up to 8 times its dry volume.

Yuzu citrus
An oriental citrus fruit whose rind has a unique aroma. Essential especially to Japanese and Korean dishes. Used when ripe and yellow in the winter and when small and green in the summer.

Yuzu-kosho pepper paste
A commercial seasoning paste made from ground *yuzu* rind, hot green chili peppers, and salt.

INQUIRIES

La Base
For purchases or questions about the kitchen tools introduced on pages 132–134, access www.labase.co.uk

index

Bold type indicates an item that is defined either in the seasonings section (pp. 136–138) or in the glossary (pp. 150–152).

Conversions

The recipes in this book use standard U.S. measures, and conversions are written in parentheses based on U.S. government guidelines. For example, in this book:

1 cup = 236. 59 ml, but is rounded up to 240 ml.
1 ounce = 28.349 g, but is rounded up to 28.5 g or 30 g

The following charts show equivalents for U.S. and metric measures. They are approximate and some recipes in this book have been converted by rounding up or down, showing different figures for easier understanding. But you do not need to be over-precise when following my recipes. Please use this chart as a reference when you need to scale the recipe for different serving amounts.

VOLUME CONVERSIONS

U.S	Metric
1/8 teaspoon	0.5 ml
1/4 teaspoon	1 ml
1/2 teaspoon	2.5 ml
3/4 teaspoon	4 ml
1 teaspoon	5 ml
1 tablespoon (3 teaspoons)	15 ml
1/4 cup (4 tablespoons)	60 ml
1/3 cup	80 ml
1/2 cup	120 ml
2/3 cup	160 ml
3/4 cup	180 ml
1 cup	240 ml
1 1/4 cups	300 ml
1 1/2 cups	360 ml
2 cups (1 pint)	480 ml
2 1/2 cups	600 ml
3 cups	720 ml
4 cups (1 quart)	1000 ml or 1 liter
1 gallon (4 quarts)	4 liters

WEIGHT CONVERSIONS

Ounces	Grams
1/4	7
1/2	15
2/3	20
1	30
1 1/2	45
2	60
2 1/2	70
3	85
3 1/2	100
4	120
5	140
6	170
7	200
8	230
9	255
10	280
11	310
12	340
14	400
16 (1 pound)	450
2 pounds	900
2 1/4 pounds	1000 g or 1 kg

LENGTH CONVERSIONS

Inches	Metric
⅛	3 mm
¼	6 mm
½	1 cm
1	2.5 cm
1½	4 cm
2	5 cm
2½	6 cm
3	7.5 cm
4	10 cm
5	13 cm
6	15 cm
8	20 cm

OVEN TEMPERATURES

Fahrenheit(°F)	Celsius (°C)	Gas Mark
250	120	½
275	130	1
300	150	2
325	160	3
340	170	3
350	180	4
375	190	5
390	200	6
410	210	3
425	220	7
450	230	8
475	245	9
500	250	10

The author and publisher would like to thank the following people for their gracious cooperation for this book:

Takeko Nakahara
Yuki Sugiura
Valerie Berry

Project coordination and editing: Noriko Yokota
Translations: Derek Wilcox and Chikako Imoto
Copy editing: Matthew Cotterill

(英文版) シンプルに食べる本
Simply Japanese

2010年1月25日　第1刷発行

著　者　有元葉子
発行者　廣田浩二
発行所　講談社インターナショナル株式会社
〒112-8652 東京都文京区音羽 1-17-14
電話 03-3944-6493（編集部）
03-3944-6492（マーケティング部・業務部）
ホームページ　www.kodansha-intl.com

印刷・製本所　大日本印刷株式会社

Printed in Japan
ISBN 978-4-7700-3102-0